POWER

IN

YOUR HAND

POWER IN YOUR HAND

by

Wallace H. Heflin, Jr.

Power In Your Hand
Copyright © 1998 — Ruth Heflin
ALL RIGHTS RESERVED

This book is protected under the copyright laws of the United States of America and may not be copied or reprinted for commercial gain or profit.

All quotations are from the Authorized King James Version of the Bible.

McDougal Publishing is a ministry of The McDougal Foundation, Inc., a Maryland nonprofit corporation dedicated to spreading the Gospel of the Lord Jesus Christ to as many people as possible in the shortest time possible.

Published by:

McDougal Publishing
P.O. Box 3595
Hagerstown, MD 21742-3595

ISBN 1-884369-60-X
(Previously ISBN 0-914903-64-0)

Printed in the United States of America
For Worldwide Distribution

Dedication

I want to dedicate these pages:

To my father, Rev. Wallace H. Heflin, Sr. He has gone to be with the Lord, but he taught us all the life of faith – how to believe and trust God despite the circumstances.

To my mother, Rev. Edith Heflin, who has been in the active ministry for more than sixty years – teaching, preaching, prophesying and challenging us to live and walk in the Spirit.

And to my sister, Rev. Ruth Heflin, who at eighteen began a missionary ministry in Hong Kong that has since blessed most every nation of the world. She now lives in Jerusalem praying and interceding for God's people, Israel.

Contents

Foreword by Harold McDougal 9
Introduction 11

1. Power In Your Hand 15
2. Such As I Have 37
3. A Man Sent By God 85
4. Availability 113

   My Prayer For You 137

Foreword

by *Harold McDougal*

This book is a compilation of four of Rev. Wallace Heflin Jr.'s most popular sermons: "Power In Your Hand," "Such As I Have," "A Man Sent By God," and "Availability." These sermons are beloved by those who were privileged to hear this great man of God in the tent revivals, campmeetings and evangelistic crusades that he conducted all across this country and around the world.

A minimum of editing has been done on the sermons, so that they retain his unique style, using short stories to reveal the point he wanted to drive home to the heart of those to whom he ministered. And they reflect some of his favorite themes, as he inspired men and women everywhere to reach out to the nations.

Those of us who knew him feel blessed and desire that many others have the opportunity to share these inspiring messages. This has been our motivation in preparing this second edition of *Power In Your Hand,* and we trust that it will be a blessing to you and yours.

Introduction

I want to speak to you through this book about the power that God has placed in your hand. If you will open yourself to God and respond to His Word, He will do something wonderful for you. He has said:

My Word ... shall not return unto Me void, but it shall accomplish that which I please, and it shall prosper in the thing whereto I sent it.
Isaiah 55:11

As believers, God has given us two ways of ministering to others. The first is with our voices. We can speak forth a "word," and that "word" can change the course of a man's life, can literally create – bring into being something that did not previously exist. We impart something through our words.

We can also impart something through our hands. There is something *very special* about YOUR hands. With your hands you can make a "point of contact," and what is in you can be given (imparted) to someone else.

God wants us to minister to others in both these ways – to speak a word and see it fulfilled and to extend a hand, touch someone, and see them healed and delivered.

Some people, who have been blessed with the laying on of hands for many years, have come to expect it and sometimes it is difficult for them to receive if someone is not there to lay hands on them. They have been conditioned to expect the laying on of hands in order to receive from God. We need to teach God's people that they can impart and receive an impartation by the spoken Word as well.

There is, however, something very special about the laying on of hands, YOUR hands. Allow God to strengthen you in this all-important ministry.

Wallace H. Heflin, Jr.
Ashland, Virginia

I beseech you therefore, brethren, by the mercies of God, that ye present your bodies a living sacrifice, holy, acceptable unto God, which is your reasonable service. And be not conformed to this world: but be ye transformed by the renewing of your mind, that ye may prove what is that good, and acceptable, and perfect, will of God.

Romans 12:1-2

Part One:

Power In Your Hand

Look At It

There is POWER IN YOUR HAND. Look at it. It may look like an ordinary piece of flesh covering some ordinary bones. Mine is white. Yours may be a different color. That hand, however, is not ordinary. I want to tell you, on the authority of the Word of God, there is POWER IN YOUR HAND.

It may be calloused. It may be worn. It may be wrinkled. It may even be dirty or greasy. But, believe me, my friend, that hand is a tool that God wants to use for ministry to give out to other men and women.

You may be a cook. If so, there is power in those hands you are cooking with. You are preparing anointed salads. You might be a stenographer. If so, you are typing anointed letters. You may be a mechanic. If you are, your hands are filled with grease; but those hands are anointed. Whatever line of work you are in, my friend, you have anointed hands.

You are called and chosen and anointed of God.

His authority and power is just lying there waiting for you to use it. God wants to use you differently than you have ever been used before.

Be Careful What You Handle

When you realize there is something special in YOUR HAND, when you begin to appreciate what God has put there, you will be more cautious about the things you handle.

I'm not talking about secular work. Don't ever be afraid or ashamed to get your hands dirty at good, honest work. I am talking about handling the sinful things of this world, the things not pleasing to God.

Years ago a sinner asked me to go to the store and buy him a pack of cigarettes. I said, "No, thank you, I don't want to have cigarettes in my hands. These hands are called and chosen and anointed of God. I don't want to touch cigarettes."

I don't want to touch a deck of cards. God delivered me from cards. I don't want to touch a whiskey bottle. God delivered me from whiskey. I don't want to allow hands that I know are chosen and anointed of God to become tools of Satan.

When you realize there is something special in YOUR hand, you will begin to experience it. Life, power and deliverance will flow out of YOUR hand. Men and women that YOU touch will be delivered and set free by the power of Almighty God.

Well publicized scandals of past years have put the spotlight on Christians and placed us all in a fish bowl. The world is forcing Christians to do what we should have been doing all the time—living a life without spot or wrinkle, a life that brings no reproach to the Gospel of Christ. We need to walk worthy of the high calling God has placed on us:

> *Therefore seeing we have this ministry, as we have received mercy, we faint not; But have renounced the hidden things of dishonesty, not walking in craftiness, nor handling the Word of God deceitfully; but by manifestation of the truth commending ourselves to every man's conscience in the sight of God. But if our Gospel be hid, it is hid to them that are lost.*
>
> 2 Corinthians 4:1-3

Many Christians have been hindering the salvation of sinners because their lives have not been what they should be before God. Paul was effective for God because he renounced the hidden things of dishonesty. Impurity and dishonesty cannot control your life if you expect to be used by God. There can be no shadow, no trace of anything that would bring reproach.

Renounce the hidden things of dishonesty. Renounce lies, black ones and white ones. Let your "yea," be yea and your "nay," nay. Do not alter the truth and make it say something it does not say.

We cannot walk in craftiness. We cannot live as others do. We must walk in holiness before God, twenty-four hours a day. Be a clean channel for Him to shine through. Let the world see Jesus shining through YOU.

We cannot handle the Word of God deceitfully. We cannot use the gifts of the Spirit for our own gain. We cannot pray special prayers for the rich and deny the poor. We cannot be dishonest financially. We have a responsibility to God, to the church and to the world. If we fail to keep that responsibility, the anointing of God will not be upon our hands. We will awaken and shake ourselves, as Samson of old, find that the Spirit of God has departed, and wonder how and when and why.

We must allow *"the manifestation of the truth"* to come forth from our lives so that we can *"commend ... ourselves to every man's conscience"* and that every man might, when he sees us, see Jesus shining through us. We must become a walking *"epistle ... known and read of all men"* (2 Corinthians 3:2). Then, others will want the glory and the anointing they see resting upon us, and the victory we enjoy.

Power In Your Hand

God has entrusted power into our hands. We are responsible to do with His power those things that will bring glory to Him. We cannot do what our own flesh wants.

"For we preach not ourselves," Paul goes on to say in that fifth verse of chapter four, *"but Christ Jesus the Lord; and ourselves your servants for Jesus' sake."* We must not so exalt the vessel that the anointing and the excellency of the power of God is lost. We must promote Jesus and remain hidden behind the cross. Then, and only then, will we see this power that God has given us be used effectively, so that the world might be shaken for His glory.

My Family's Experience

Many years ago my sister, Ruth, was helping the cooks in the old, original kitchen of our camp. She was mixing salad. She had the tomatoes, the lettuce, the celery, the mayonnaise etc., all in a big salad bowl. Because there were so many people to be fed, she couldn't mix the salad with a couple of forks. She had to toss it with her hands. She had mayonnaise between her fingers, lettuce on the back of her hand and tomato juice up to her elbow.

Suddenly, the door opened and two ladies entered. One of them said, "This sister is very sick. She needs prayer." Ruth scraped the largest pieces of salad off her hands and arms, wiped her hands quickly on her apron, approached the sister and laid her hands on her. She commanded her to be healed. The woman "fell out" under the power of God on that concrete floor. When she got up she was healed.

Ministry In India

In 1961 and 1962, my father, mother and sister went to India together. They were taken to a village where a little, five-year-old girl who had never walked was taken to their meetings. My father took the little Indian girl in his arms, lifted her up to God, and began to pray for her healing. As he was praying, he took ten or twelve steps backward–away from the mother. That little girl was terribly frightened by this strange-looking man. She began to cry loudly. She wanted to go back to Mother. Dad continued to hold her tight in his arms until she began to kick those legs that had not moved well. She screamed. She wanted to go back to Mother. When he released her, she ran to her mother–healed by the power of God. My father said that the following night there were several hundred mothers holding children that needed to be prayed for.

I never forgot that story. The first time I had occasion to pray for a baby that had never walked a step in her life, I remembered how Dad had done it. I took that young child in my arms as he had, held it up to God as he had, and backed away from the mother as he had. Sure enough, when the child saw my strange face, she wanted to go home. When I put her back down on the floor, she too ran–healed by God's power.

I have laid my hands on many children that have never walked before and God has done the work. What happened? God extended His hand with mine. YOUR hand is the extension of the hand of God. When you extend your hand, Jesus extends His hand. His hand on top of YOUR hand brings the necessary miracle.

I Have Tasted It

In 1969 we conducted a tent revival in Richmond. At the back of the tent one night was an unsaved man with his wife and two daughters. After preaching on Heaven, I went back to try to get him to the altar, but he wouldn't go.

I wanted to get my hands on that man any way I could. I knew that if I got my hands on him he would feel God's power. I said to him, "Let me pray for you. Let me pray for God to bless you." (Everybody likes to get blessed.) He extended his hand to me. I put my big hand in his and began to pray. And God began to move.

He said later that after I began to pray, if he could have gotten his hand out of "that preacher's" hand, he would have left "that tent" quickly. But it was too late. The power of the Holy Ghost went out of me and into him. Before the meeting was over, God saved and baptized him, his wife and two teenage daughters in the Holy Ghost.

God healed the oldest daughter. She was the fifth baby to be born and the first one to live. Her eyes had been operated on three times. She could not see letters that were nearly an inch high. One of her legs was shorter than the other. One foot was two shoe sizes smaller than the other one. In a moment's time, Jesus restored her vision and took the limp out of her leg.

When she went to school the next day, the teacher asked, "What happened? You're not limping anymore."

"I went to the Pentecostal tent meeting," she answered. "The preacher laid his hand on me."

There is life and power and deliverance in YOUR hand as well.

An Elder With Cancer

In 1978 I was preaching in a church in Queensland, Australia. One of the elders of the church had developed cancer of the face from shrapnel wounds sustained in the Second World War. I have never seen a more terrible looking face in my life. There was not one spot on his face that was not raw with cancer. He had several large cancers under his neck. His ear was eaten with cancer, and when anyone touched it, he thought he would go out of his mind with pain. Doctors had examined him several days before and had told him to prepare for the end, for it would not be long in coming.

I was in that church for only two nights. The first night I didn't pray for him. In the afternoon of the second day, while I was praying, I saw myself putting my hands on that man's cancerous face. The devil said to me, "You're not going to put your hands on those cancers are you?"

At first I wondered even why the man came to church. He was the usher at the door. Everyone who came in the door had to look at him. Then I began to realize what suffering and misery he must be going through, what an effort he had put forth, even to come to the House of God. He was exercising his faith.

I was sure that he had been prayed for many times before, so I said to the people that night, "I want you to act as though this is the first time you have ever seen this man." I said to him, "I want you to act as though this is the first time you have ever been prayed for. I am going to put my hands on you."

I stretched my big hands over that man's face and covered every part of the cancer I could. I cursed the cancer in the Name of Jesus. As I did this, the power of God went through the man. When I opened my eyes, I saw a color change in his face.

I said to him, "Touch your face."

He began to touch his skin. He pulled his ear. He said, "Preacher, if I would have done that before, I'd have gone out of my mind with pain. But I have no pain. God has taken all my pain." He was delivered by the power of Almighty God.

That was nine o'clock at night. The service was over about twelve midnight. I looked for him to examine his face again.

The pastor said to me, "Look, there is another color change in his face."

I said, "Brother, would you just touch your face one more time. I want to see what God has done."

He pressed his fingers around various parts of his face and could not find a sign of pain.

Four or five nights later two of the young people came one hundred and fifty miles to another meeting that we were in. I asked them, "How is that Brother?"

"He's still healed," was their reply.

YOUR hands too are anointed of God. They can produce miracles. God has anointed YOUR hands so that miracles shall flow out of YOU—so that the lives of men and women shall be shaken by the power of Almighty God. There is life in YOUR hand.

Position Your Hands Correctly

Most of us have our hands turned face up to God—in a position to receive. We are always reaching out for ourselves. "I will just get a little more for myself and be sure my family is taken care of." But it is still *"more blessed to give than to receive."* The Holy Ghost is raising up men and women today who are willing to turn that hand over and use it to give—not just to get.

Use your hand to give out joy. Give out peace. Give tenderness. Give authority in God. Give out healing. Take what God has given you and share it with someone else. The Lord wants you to turn your hand over and minister to the crying needs of humanity.

Pass the Bread, Please

Many years ago a Spirit-filled Methodist brother from North Carolina came to conduct a meeting in our church. I will never forget the story that he told us:

Power In Your Hand

Tape recorders were just becoming popular. A certain man bought a tape recorder, and he and his wife decided to have some fun with their children. They hid the recorder under the kitchen table, encouraged a lively conversation, and later played it all back in the living room to see the children's surprise.

Conversation was going nicely around the table. Everyone was laughing. Suddenly, the smallest girl shouted out, "PASS THE BREAD, PLEASE."

The father got so upset that he said, "Young lady, what in the world do you think you are doing hollering like that? Now, get down from the table and go to your room without your dinner."

Crying like her heart would break, she padded down the hall, went into her room and shut the door. Later in the evening they brought out the tape recorder as planned. Everyone gathered around it in the living room, and they began replaying the mealtime conversation.

After awhile they heard on the tape a tiny voice saying, "Pass the bread, please," then, "Pass the bread, please," and again, "Pass the bread please." When no one responded, the volume rose until it became the shout that had startled everyone. The child had been asking for bread, but because everyone was so busy "doing their own thing," they had not heard her cry.

Power In Your Hand

The father felt so badly. He had punished his daughter and sent her to bed without her dinner. He ran to her room, grabbed her up in his arms, and apologized to her. She had been asking properly. It was he who had been so busy he had no time for her need.

Much of the church world has gotten so busy "doing it's own thing" that we sometimes cannot hear the cries of those who are begging for our help. They need someone to give them the Bread of Life, someone to minister to them, that they might be delivered and set free by the power of Almighty God. Friends, it is time to stir ourselves.

When the power and authority of God is within us, we must not let it lie dormant. We cannot sit idly by when we have that which is necessary to bring deliverance to a world that is lost without God.

The Word declares:

> *Withhold not good from them to whom it is due, when it is in the power of THINE HAND to do it.* Proverbs 3:27

Examples From the Word of God

The Word of God is filled with examples of what happened when hands were laid on people:

Power In Your Hand

Joshua ... was full of ... wisdom; for Moses had laid HIS HANDS upon him.
                              Deuteronomy 34:9

The wisdom that Joshua needed to take over the monumental task of leading God's people into the promised land was imparted to him through the laying on of hands.

Paul, in writing to Timothy, said:

[Timothy], neglect not the gift that is in thee, which was given thee by prophecy, with THE LAYING ON OF THE HANDS of the presbytery.   1 Timothy 4:14

Stir up the gift of God, which is in thee BY THE PUTTING ON OF MY HANDS.
                              2 Timothy 1:6

Timothy was never the same after the laying on of hands. Something was imparted to him. He received a *"gift."*

When Isaac was getting old and too blind to tell his two sons apart, Jacob deceived him. He put goat skins on his hands and neck to make himself seem hairy like Esau, his older brother.

Isaac asked him:

Power In Your Hand

Who art thou, my son? Genesis 27:18

Jacob answered:

I am Esau, thy firstborn. Verse 19

His father was skeptical:

Come near ... that I may feel thee.
　　　　　　　　　　　　　　Verse 21

Jacob obeyed, but Isaac was not satisfied:

The voice is Jacob's voice, but the hands are the hands of Esau. Verse 22

Isaac was deceived, laid his hands on Jacob and gave to him the paternal blessing that belonged rightfully to Esau.

Jacob knew there was something so wonderful in the hands of an old blind man that he was willing to be deceptive to get it.

When soldiers came to take Jesus captive in the Garden of Gethsemane, the first thing they did was to bind His hands. Those hands had made mud, placed it on the eyes of a blind man and healed him of his blindness. Those hands had gathered the children tenderly to the Master's side. Those hands stopped a funeral procession in Nain, opened the coffin of a young boy and gave him new life. Those were the hands that blessed and broke the bread that fed the multitudes. Those hands had been laid upon great masses of sick and suffering, helpless and incurable people that followed Him. Healing and deliverance had come so that now Jesus' enemies recognized that they must first bind those miracle-working hands.

If the devil can bind your hands, he can keep you from doing the work of God. If he can convince you there is nothing different about your hands and can thus keep you from using them, he has you right where he wants you. If, on the other hand, you will begin to use the hands God has given you, life and deliverance will flow forth from them.

Physical Exertion

The hand is an instrument that God has chosen to use—to pour forth blessing upon the people around you. When we use our hands, however, we have to exert some energy. Many believers don't want to work for God. If anything like work is involved, count them out. They want to take the easy way out. But God has given us hands to work with.

The Bible says:

Power In Your Hand

The harvest truly is great, but the labourers are few: pray ye therefore the Lord of the harvest, that He would send forth LABOURERS into His harvest. Luke 10:2

God is looking for laborers to go into the fields and reap the whitened harvest—using, physically and spiritually, the hands that He has given them.

Don't be afraid of work. If you are diligent to work with your hands, the anointing of God will be increased upon your soul, and wherever you go, God will give you victory.

Often we say one thing with our mouths, but do another thing with our hands. The Bible says:

Whatsoever thy hand findeth to do, DO IT with thy might. Ecclesiastes 9:10

No man, having put HIS HAND to the plough, and looking back, is fit for the kingdom of God. Luke 9:62

Spiritual Jealousy

Some folks won't work for God unless they can be "number one." God is looking for men and women today that will be faithful to hold up the hands of others. There is a ministry in holding up the hands of our brothers and sisters. Far too long there has been spiritual jealousy in the Body of Christ.

Spiritual jealousy is worse than political jealousy. Many politicians cut each others' throats. They don't care what they do or say–just as long as they get elected. In many circles spiritual jealousy has gotten just as bad. It has destroyed characters and lives and entire ministries.

Jealousy is insecurity. Thank God that in the present day move of His Spirit, jealousy is being done away with. God is finding men and women willing to hold up someone else's hands.

It really makes no difference who does the preaching–just so the Word gets preached. It makes no difference who does the laying on of hands–just so we get people healed and delivered. It makes no difference who does the prophesying–just so it is done. God is raising up men and women with power and authority and a willingness to hold up the hands of another.

It is time that we encourage our brethren and strengthen them for the battle that lies ahead. We are in a warfare, my friend.

When you become sensitive enough to see your brother's need and when you open your *"bowels of compassion"* to him, then the power of God will be increased in your own soul. When you see your

Power In Your Hand

brother fallen and you reach down and pick him up, everyone will recognize that you have grown in God. And God will bless you. You will find the anointing more rich upon your soul.

The Bible gives us a beautiful example in the life of Moses: Battle was raging between the children of Israel and the Amalekites. Moses went to a mountain overlooking the scene. There he held his hands up to God–as a sign of surrender to His will and as an invocation to God to come and fight their mutual enemies. As long as the hands of Moses were uplifted the children of Israel did well in the battle; but when Moses got tired and his arms began to sag, the enemy prevailed.

When Aaron and Hur saw what was happening, one of them got on one side of Moses and the other got on the other side, and they held up his hands until the battle was won.

Where are the Aarons and the Hurs? We still need to hold up the hands of our brothers and sisters today. Forget what denomination you belong to. Forget what name is on the front of the church building. Forget doctrinal background. If someone is preaching the Word of God–the death, resurrection and soon coming of Jesus–you and I need to stand and hold up his hands so that the enemy cannot defeat him, so that doors cannot be closed to him, and so that he is not discouraged in the way. If we can hold up his hands for awhile, he will be strengthened to continue the work that God has called him to do.

When we are willing to strengthen someone else, God will strengthen us. When we, however, have no concern for others, when it is dog eat dog, everyone for themselves, crawl all over the other one, and push him down in order to succeed, we lose the very thing that our soul cries and longs for–the blessing of God.

Part Two:
Such As I Have

Peter Had Something Worth Giving

Then Peter said, Silver and gold have I none; but SUCH AS I HAVE give I thee: In the name of Jesus Christ of Nazareth rise up and walk. And he took him by the right hand, and lifted him up: and immediately his feet and ankle bones received strength. And he leaping up stood, and walked, and entered with them into the temple, walking, and leaping, and praising God. Acts 3:6-8

God uses what is in our hands. Sometimes we look at our meager possessions and say, "Lord, what is this?"

God replies, "That's all I need."

It's interesting. The Lord always wants us to recognize our nothingness. He wants us to recognize how little we have—to make us more dependent on Him. When we see our nothingness or the "littleness" of what we have and we know that the need is great, we throw ourselves upon the mercies of God. Then God puts His big hand upon our little hand, and that little bit that we have begins to grow and multiply until the need is met. We are always astounded at what God does. He does it because we use what is in our hands.

The devil has told you that you have nothing of value; but he is a liar, my friend. You have anointing. You have life. You have power. And it is all in your hand. There is resurrection power in your hand. There is healing power in your hand.

The Widows of the Old Testament

The widow of Zarephath had only a little meal and a little oil. She and her son were going to eat the last cake and die. Instead, she gave it to God. God put His hand on the little that she had and multiplied it. It lasted for three and a half years (1 Kings 17:8-16).

What about the widow that lost her husband and was about to lose her sons because she could not pay her creditors? She went to Elisha the prophet for help. He asked her what she had left in the house. She replied that all she had left of value was a pot of oil. But that was enough. God showed her how to use what she had to pay the entire debt, save her sons, and still have enough left over to live on (2 Kings 4:1-7).

Such As I Have

As that little widow shut her door and began to pour out the little bit of oil that she had, it kept pouring and pouring. It did not run out until every last vessel that she had been able to borrow was filled. God used what she had to meet the need.

The Disciples Fed A Multitude

One day Jesus asked the disciples where they could buy enough bread to feed five thousand people. Andrew came saying that a small lad had volunteered his lunch, but it contained only five small barley rolls and two small fish. He asked:

But what are they among so many? John 6:9

Jesus told them to seat the people so they could eat and to bring what they had to Him. He put His hand upon it and blessed it; and, in so doing, He multiplied it. He gave it to the disciples and they, in turn, served it to the multitude.

I don't believe however, that Jesus divided the bread and the fish until there were fifteen or twenty thousand pieces of each. I believe that He broke the loaves until there were twelve. He broke the fish until there were twelve. He gave a piece of fish, and He gave a piece of bread to each of the disciples. Then He told them to feed the multitude.

Give ye them to eat.   Matthew 14:16

What each disciple had in his hand was still insufficient; but as they all, in obedience, began to give out what they had, the miracle took place. To their amazement, their "little" fed five thousand. Maybe the greatest miracle was that when everyone had eaten, each one of the twelve had a basketful left over (John 6:5-13). Praise God!

As you begin to use what is already in your hand, you will find that the anointing is sufficient. The delivering power of God shall be present, and the work shall be done for God.

Moses Had A Rod

What God has already given you is sufficient for the hour. All that He wants is for you to do His will. God said to Moses on the back side of the desert:

What is that in thine hand?   Exodus 4:2

Moses answered:

[Just an old, dead stick]—a rod.   Verse 2

God said:

Such As I Have

[Throw it down]—Cast it on the ground.
Verse 3

When Moses threw it down, the rod became a serpent. Then the Lord said:

[Now], take it by the tail.   Verse 4

When Moses obeyed, the snake became a rod again in his hand. It was a rod all the time. But Moses needed to discover the power in his hand. He wasn't yet aware of the magnitude of the power and the authority he had. You and I need to know that God has given us the authority—not just that He will give it to us. He has already given it to us. The power is in YOUR hand. If you will say, "God, I want these hands to be used of Thee," YOUR hands will bring life and deliverance to a lost and dying world.

When Moses got to the Red Sea with nowhere to go, God said to him:

Stretch out thine hand over the sea, and divide it.   Exodus 14:16

Moses obeyed, and the children of Israel were able to cross over on dry ground. The God of Moses has not changed. Let Him use whatever you happen to have in your hand today.

The Importance of the House of God

One of the most powerful examples of this happened in the first century church and is recorded in Acts 3. I think we are all familiar with this Scriptural story that took place just days after the outpouring of the Holy Ghost on the Day of Pentecost.

The chapter begins by saying that Peter and John went up to the Temple *"at the hour of prayer"* (Verse 1). The disciples didn't "get it all" when they got baptized in the Holy Ghost. They still needed to go to the House of God. Many people these days speak a few words in tongues and then sit back and say, "Bless God! We got it all! We got our tongue and we don't need any more." Speaking in tongues, however, is just the key to unlock the treasure chest of Heaven. You must continue to persevere.

Even the Apostle Paul said:

> *Not [that I have] already obtained ... but ... I press toward the mark for the prize of the high calling of God in Christ Jesus.*
> Philippians 3:12-14

Such As I Have

Thank God for the example that Peter and John set for every one of us. When we get to the place that we no longer want to go to the House of God, we are in trouble spiritually.

There is a teaching circulating these days in some circles that it is not really necessary to go to church. But the Bible says clearly:

> *Not forsaking the assembling of ourselves together, as the manner of some is; but exhorting one another: and so much the more, as ye see the day approaching.* Hebrews 10:25

David said:

> *I was glad when they said unto me, 'Let us go into the house of the Lord.'* Psalm 122:1

There is a definite need for people to go the House of the Lord. We need fellowship. We need to come together with the Saints of God. We need to feel that anointing that flows from one another. We need to draw strength from one another. We need to see that we are not alone in living this new life in Jesus. We need to know that others are rejoicing and enjoying the blessings of God. We must receive so that we can have something to give to others.

Power In Your Hand

Minister Wherever You Find Needy People

Peter and John were going to church. As they were going to church, they saw a man that was sick. It is interesting that this man was outside the church. He wasn't in the Temple. He was outside the Temple. Too many people feel that the only time you can pray for the sick is when you are in the church. You can pray for the sick on the street corner or anywhere else for that matter. Most of them are not in the church!

One brother was standing on the street corner. He had a word of knowledge ministry. As people came across the street toward him, God was showing him what was wrong with them. He stopped them as they reached the sidewalk and said, "The Lord showed me that you have [such and such ache]. I'll pray for you right here if you'd like." He was praying for them on the street corner. Well, that is what Peter and John were doing.

The lame man was crippled *"from his mother's womb."* They *"laid"* him *"daily at the gate of the Temple"* (Acts 3:2). I am sure that Peter and John had seen him often. He was there every day, and they went there to pray every day. But this time there was a difference. The difference was not in the crippled man. The difference was in Peter and

John. Something had happened to them just a day or two before. They had something new, something to give out to others. Praise God!

A Beggar No More

The man was expecting some money. That was the way he made his living. There were professional beggars in those days, just as there are professional beggars throughout the world today. They even wore the garment of a beggar in Bible days.

Remember blind Bartimaeus? He wore a beggar's garment. It identified him as a blind person and a beggar. When Jesus called blind Bartimaeus to come to Him, he whipped off that garment (Mark 10:49-50). He wasn't planning to beg anymore. He knew that Jesus would heal him. He wouldn't need to beg.

The man that Peter and John met at the Beautiful Gate also made his living by begging. But Peter said to him:

> *Silver and gold have I none; but SUCH AS I HAVE give I thee:*   Acts 3:6

And when Peter ministered to the lame man what he had received from God, that man's life was forever changed.

I am talking to you about what you have, not what you will have. I am talking about what you have now, not what you will get next week, next month or next year. I am talking to you about the power and the faith that is already inside YOU. I want to stir it up, that, by the time you finish reading this book, you will be moving in a realm of faith and anointing that you were not moving in when you picked it up.

Avoid Spiritual Weariness

I sense that many of God's people are becoming weary of the journey, and that because of the weariness, they are not in the proper attitude of faith to possess the promises of God. The Bible says:

Let us not be weary in well doing: for in due season we shall reap, if we faint not.
Galatians 6:9

This is not a time for weariness. This is a time to let your faith be released. We must not allow the things of the natural to bind and tie us and take our mind and our eyes off the vision and the promise that God has given to us. We must stand firmer than ever before, and say, "I am going to lay claim

to that which the Lord has spoken."
The Scriptures say:

> *For ye have need of patience, that, after ye have done the will of God, ye might receive the promise.* Hebrews 10:36

Hold on tight to what God has given you.

A Time For Faith

We sing about faith and talk about faith. Now it is time we acted in faith. Faith is not moved by what it sees. Faith is not moved by what it hears. Faith is moved only by the Word of God–which never changes:

> *Heaven and earth shall pass away, but My Words shall not pass away.* Matthew 24:35

We can stand on the authority of God's unchanging Word and know that He will keep the promise that He has made us.

Peter first said to the man, *"Look on us"* (Acts 3:4). If you have the confidence and the faith of God within your soul, you too can say, "Look on us." You know what God will do through YOU.

Power In Your Hand

The Holy Ghost has given YOU the power and the authority to lay YOUR hands on the heads of men and women bound by the powers of Satan and see them delivered. God is looking for somebody today that will dare to stand and say, *"Such as I have"* and *"Look on [me]."*

I am not talking about a boastful spirit. If you become boastful, the anointing will begin to slip away from you. I am talking about the confidence you have that your God is a Healer, that what He has placed in you is sufficient.

The Scriptures say that Jesus *"healed them all"* (Matthew 12:15). He ministered to the multitudes and "HE HEALED THEM ALL." The Gospel of John goes on to say that if all the miracles that Jesus did were recorded, there would not be enough books in the whole world to contain them (John 21:25). Amen!

Can you picture that multitude of people that followed Jesus? HE HEALED THEM ALL. What if every one of them would have testified a little bit?

"I was born with a deformity. I am normal now."

"I was born blind. I see everything."

"I was deaf. I can hear everything He is saying."

"I had a congenital heart condition. It is healed."

Jesus just spoke the Word and brought healing! Jesus brought deliverance. Jesus set them free. HE HEALED THEM ALL!

Such As I Have

The disciples of John came to inquire of Jesus:

Art thou He that should come, or do we look for another? Matthew 11:3

Jesus answered:

Go and shew John ... the blind receive their sight, the lame walk, the lepers are cleansed, and the deaf hear, the dead are raised up, and the poor have the gospel preached to them.
Matthew 11:4-5

Healing today is a sign of Christ's present and continuing glory and power. He is still working, still performing miracles. Thank God that He is The Healer–today. Thank God that He is The Miracle-working God–still. And He is doing it through the anointed hands of His servants. Use what is in your hand.

You Need Signs Following You

Peter said, *"Look on us."* I want you to have that same testimony. I want you to know there is power and authority in YOUR hands. I want you to know that YOU can stretch forth YOUR hands and do the work of God.

Power In Your Hand

Jesus said:

*These signs shall follow them that believe; ...
They shall lay hands on the sick, and they shall
recover.* Mark 16:17-18

Who is the *"they"* in that verse? Put yourself there in place of the *"they."* *"[YOU] shall lay hands on the sick, and they shall recover."*

Many believers spend their time chasing across the country following the signs of some great evangelist, but every one of us should be producing some signs and some wonders for God. If you are willing to stretch forth your hand, you can fulfill the Great Commission. You have something to offer.

Peter said, *"Such as I have give I unto thee."* May you have such faith in the power that God has given to you that you shall say, "SUCH AS I HAVE," and give it to someone.

God Healed A Broken Arm

Some years ago, a sister from Tennessee went with me on a trip to the Holy Land. Seven or eight days before she was to get on the plane she broke her wrist. When she got on the plane her right arm

Such As I Have

was in a cast and the cast was in a sling. Others had to carry her bag and help her cut her food and get around.

There was also a doctor from Australia with us on the tour. When he first arrived in Israel he told me, "I brought my little black bag." I didn't really believe him. I thought he was just joking. He wasn't.

He said, "I have been to so many conventions where they asked, 'Is there a doctor in the house?' 'Is there a doctor on the plane?' So I brought my black bag just in case."

He was a good, open, spirit-filled brother that God was using; and, during the seven or eight days we were together in Israel, we talked together much about miracles and healing.

He asked me, "What would you do if somebody with you on the tour broke a bone?"

I said, "My first reaction would be to pray for them. That's all I know."

A couple of days before we were to disband and return to our homes, we went to breakfast one morning in the hotel, only to find that several people had not come down because they were sick. So, the preacher and the doctor went together to make house calls.

We went to the first room and knocked on the door. I said, "We've both come. Take your pick.

You can either have his prescription or mine. Mine works the fastest."

Each one chose my remedy. We laid hands on those sick folk, and in a few minutes time they were all down to breakfast.

That night we had a meeting. I felt led to call the sister with the broken arm to the front and pray for her. She came forward with the arm in the sling. I called the doctor up to pray with me.

I said, "We are going to pray for God to bring deliverance to her." When we finished praying the power of God hit her and she began rejoicing, shouting and dancing. I knew that God had healed her. "How does it feel?" I asked her.

She said, "The pain is gone!"

I said, "Check that arm, Doc."

He grasped her elbow with one hand and her wrist with the other and started jerking. I thought he would break it again. He wanted to be sure that the arm was healed. It was! And it still is! Our God is a miracle-working God!

Power From Heaven

You must realize that it is the miraculous power of God that will work for you. When you believe it, something will happen.

Such As I Have

Peter knew that he received something that he had never had before. Jesus had said to him:

Tarry ye in the city of Jerusalem, until ye be endued with power from on high.
Luke 24:49

What Peter received didn't come from "the Pentecostal Church." It didn't come from "headquarters." It didn't come from an "organization." It came from Heaven. Hallelujah! And Peter knew he had received something that he did not have before.

So many people today say, "I will pray for you, but if God doesn't do the work, if He doesn't come, you won't get anything. There is nothing in me. If God wants to heal you, He will heal you."

Well, if you don't believe you have anything, please don't give it to me. I want somebody to lay hands on me that has something in his hands, something in his soul, and knows that he has it.

Elisha Had Something That He Imparted To Naaman

I love the story of Naaman. He was Captain of the Syrian armies, but he had leprosy. His king sent him to Israel, in the hope that he could find healing there. He carried a letter of introduction to the King of Israel.

When he arrived at his destination and presented his letter of introduction, the King of Israel was very upset. He knew that he had nothing to offer the man. He said:

> *Am I God ... to recover a man of his leprosy?*
> 2 Kings 5:7

When Elisha heard about it, he said:

> *Let him come now to me, and he shall know that there is a prophet in Israel.* Verse 8

God wants to raise up some prophets in America. He wants the world to know that YOU have power, YOU have faith, and YOU have authority in God.

Why? Because these are the last days. We need signs and wonders to shake men and women and make them realize that Jesus is still alive, alive in YOU!

Acting on Your Faith

When Peter said, *"Look on us,"* it must have

Such As I Have

startled that crippled man. Then he said, *"SUCH AS I HAVE."* But not only did he say, *"Look on us,"* and *"Such as I have,"* he put his faith to work. He reached down, took the man by the hand, and pulled him to his feet. He could have gone on to prayer and left the man sitting there. If he had, however, the man probably could not have received his miracle from God.

It takes more faith to act upon your prayers. But Peter knew he had something. When you are praying for someone that is severely ill, don't leave them without finding out what God has done in answer to your prayer.

The devil will tell you, "Doing that might put you 'on the spot.' Suppose the pain is not gone. Suppose they still can't move that arm. Suppose they still can't wiggle that toe. Suppose the condition hasn't left yet. What will it do to your reputation?"

Forget your reputation. Let your faith be exercised, and let the Name of Jesus be glorified. Jesus is the Healer. It is Jesus Who will do the work. He is the miracle-working God. When we dare take a man by the hand and pull him to his feet, we will see the power of God flow through him. That man will be delivered. God's Word declares it to be so.

Power In Your Hand

Dr. Raj, Meet Dr. Jesus!

In September of 1970, I was in meetings in India. I was staying in the home of Dr. Joshua Raj, a medical doctor for twenty years. One day he came into the living room where I was and said, "There is a man outside that wants to be prayed for."

I said, "Why don't you let him wait for the service. We'll pray for him there."

He said, "He just left the hospital. He has been given only a one-hour leave of absence. Two years ago he was bitten by a dog. They gave him a dozen rabies shots that left him paralyzed from the waist down."

I put my shoes on and went outside where the young Hindu man, from a very prominent family, was waiting in a three-wheeled taxi. We took a chair, helped get him out, set him in the middle of the street, and laid hands on him. We rebuked that condition in the Name of Jesus.

But we didn't leave him in the chair or send him away immediately. We took him by the hand and pulled him to his feet. He started walking up and down that street. He was healed by the power of Almighty God. He went back to the hospital where they gave him a thorough examination, pronounced him "cured," and dismissed him.

Such As I Have

During that same meeting we prayed for a three year old boy that had never walked a step in his life. He was healed.

Dr. Raj saw those miracles. Although he was a medical doctor for twenty years, he was also doing some preaching. Now the Lord spoke to him through prophecy to make a greater commitment. His response was, "God, if You will give me ninety days to close my practice, I'll devote my full time to the ministry." Ninety days later he closed the dispensary. Today there is a Pentecostal Church where he used to dispense the pills. He learned that God's power is greater than the power of mortals. When you and I put our necks on the line, Jesus comes and honors our faith. Don't worry about your reputation.

Believe For Miracles

You have been telling God that you are willing to go where He wants to send you. You have been getting yourself ready. Don't let doubts and unbelief come in now. Stand strong in faith, being fully persuaded that the One that spoke and the One that promised is able to perform His Word. Even when it looks impossible, my Jesus will be there to work for you. Amen!

Miracles are something you can't do for yourself. Believe Him! He will do the miracles for you!

During another tour of India, I was asked to pray for a retired postmaster who had suffered a stroke and was bedridden. He was from a prominent Muslim family.

I said to him, "Jesus is the Son of God. He is alive, and one of the ways He proves it is by performing miracles."

Moslems do not believe that Jesus is the Son of God. I am sure that man could have argued eloquently with what I said. He replied simply, "We will see."

After prayer we pulled him to his feet and two of us started walking him across the floor. He was able to straighten his knees and walk for the first time in two years. I didn't have to repeat to him that Jesus was the Son of God and alive. He knew it now.

Holiness And Power Go Together

You already know what happened to the lame man at the Beautiful Gate. After he had a time of walking, leaping, and praising God, he took hold of Peter and John. The Scripture say:

Such As I Have

The lame man which was healed held Peter and John.   Acts 3:11

Peter decided that it was a good time to preach a little sermon. He was led to say:

Ye men of Israel, why marvel ye at this? or why look ye so earnestly on us, as though by our own power or holiness we had made this man to walk.   Verse 12

Notice that he put power and holiness together. If you want to have power with God, you must move into a life of holiness. If you don't move into a life of holiness, you will never have power with God. The two go together.

When people stop living a life of holiness and sanctification (you can't tell the saints from the sinners anymore), they lose their power and have to make excuses. They say, "God's not healing that way anymore."

I want to tell you: you and I are about to see the greatest miracles that the church world has ever seen. Miracles will not diminish. They will be more astounding every day that goes by. We will live in the realm of the anointing; and God will give us miracles greater than anything that we have ever experienced before–because we are quickly approaching the Second Coming of Jesus.

We will see more creative miracles. They will come more easily and more quickly and be more astounding than ever, and sinners will come to God as they see His power through us.

The Amazing Story of Ronald Coyne

Some of the readers may have heard of Ronald Coyne. What a tremendous miracle God has given him! He lost an eye as a child and had to wear a plastic eye. But God has given him sight in that eye socket. He can take the plastic eyeball out, set it on the pulpit and read anything that you give him to read–with no eyeball. He has been experiencing this miracle now for nearly forty years. Teams of doctors have examined him and they could find no logical explanation for this miracle.

There is an explanation. Let me introduce you to my private Physician. Everyone should have one. His name is JESUS! He is not just the God of Ronald Coyne. He will do the same for anybody foolish enough to dare to lay hands on the sick, believing for a miracle.

Coming Revival

We are on the verge of great revival. God said He

would give us the former rain and the latter rain. He will combine them and give them to us in the same month. We will see unusual manifestations of God not even recorded in the book of Acts. God will give His people signs and wonders and miracles as they begin to proclaim the soon return of our Lord and Savior, Jesus Christ.

I am a candidate today for greater miracles. How about you? Do you want God to use you? Do you want God to work through your life? He is looking for willing vessels. Just say "yes" to Him.

His Name

Peter said to the people gathered that day in Jerusalem:

> *And His name through faith in His name hath made this man strong, whom ye see and know: yea, the faith which is by Him hath given him this perfect soundness in the presence of you all.* Acts 3:16

What a powerful portion of scripture. Oh, praise God! It is His name and faith in His name that will get the job done. Peter was absolutely right. Friends, there is no other name that can compare:

Power In Your Hand

There is none other name ... given among men, whereby we must be saved.   Act 4:12

You can pray to Krishna and Shiva and all the three hundred and thirty million gods of India and nothing will happen. But when you begin to lift your voice in prayer in the name of Jesus, the forces of Heaven are called to your side, and a miracle takes place. Dare to believe and stand upon the promises of God.

Two Hundred Miles A Day

In a meeting that I had in Nambour, Queensland, Australia a woman drove fifty miles for the morning service and went back home when it was over. She drove fifty miles for the night service and drove back afterward. That woman drove almost two hundred miles every day for the sixteen days that I was there. Not only did she come herself, but every time she came she brought at least one car load of people and sometimes two and three.

Somebody asked her, "Why are you driving two hundred miles every day with the shortage of gasoline and its high price?"

She answered, "Two years ago Brother Heflin came to the small church in our home town. I had a water leg. The doctor told me I would be that way all my life. I could hardly stand on that leg. It was swollen and infected.

"Brother Heflin prayed for me in the name of Jesus. When he finished praying, he told me to run toward the door. As I got to the door, I felt the power of God go through me. My leg is perfectly whole. I am coming to give glory to Jesus for the miracle He has given me."

Friend, the world is dying for someone to tell them that Jesus is not dead. He is alive. His name is powerful! Faith in His name produces miracles! When we pray in the name of Jesus something happens.

The Blackest Sinner, Saved and Healed

Once, when we were in India, we had ordered a tent made. The tent got lost in transit, so we began some open-air meetings while we waited for it. By rigging some lights across an open field, we were able to have several nights of meetings. Large numbers attended and all sorts of miracles took place.

The tent finally arrived. The morning the tent was being raised a Hindu woman, who had known nothing about Jesus, came with her mother and her four-year-old daughter. Some pastors had been telling her what was happening in the open-air meetings and she was believing God for a miracle.

When her baby was born something happened to damage a nerve in the woman's hip. She had not been able to walk properly for the past four years.

An Indian pastor led the woman to Jesus. In doing so, he told her his own testimony. He said, "I was the blackest sinner that ever lived. Jesus came and took my sins away and changed my life."

Tears streamed down that woman's face and she was shaking her head and replying something to him. I asked another pastor who was there to interpret to me what she was saying.

"She is saying, 'You could not have been the blackest sinner that ever lived. I am.'"

We prayed for that woman's healing. After I prayed, I asked her to run across the field. Remember, she had been dragging one leg for four years. She started running. She was able to run and rejoice. When she came back, I asked her to run again. She did. God had come upon her and she was completely healed.

When she returned the second time, I noticed that she was digging down into her sari, searching for something. I could hear her saying over and over the name of Jesus in her dialect, but I couldn't understand what she was looking for. I asked the interpreter what she was doing.

He said, "She is looking for a pencil and paper. She wants to write down the name of Jesus. She is saying, 'I don't want to forget His name! My leg is healed. My life is changed. Tell me His name one more time.' "

You too have power. Use it.

His Name Is Powerful

Several years ago, we were traveling from the Sea of Galilee to Nablus, where Jacob's well is located. It started to rain lightly as we entered the city. That first rain of the year combined with the dust and oil of the road to form a very slippery surface.

I had been asleep for a few minutes, and when I awoke, I saw, as we started around a curve in the road, a store on one side with two children standing in front of it. The wheels of the bus lost traction and, with forty-five of us inside, that heavy bus began to slide toward the children and the store building.

I whispered, "Jesus!"

The bus kept sliding.

Louder this time, I said, "Jesus!"

There seemed to be no possible way of keeping that big bus from going right through that building, killing the two children, and injuring many of our people.

I cried out with all my strength, "JESUS!"

When I did that, the bus stopped as though it had hit a wall. The front was already past the curb. The two children stood petrified with fright just a few feet in front of us. The bus had to back up to get back into the street.

Both our driver and our guide were Muslims. When we got back to Jerusalem, they spread the word throughout the city, "Rev. Heflin prayed in the name of Jesus, and Jesus stopped the bus."

He is no respecter of persons. If YOU believe, YOU will see God move in YOUR behalf. As Peter said, It's "His name" and "faith in His name," that does the work. Use the authority He has given you.

Tommy Osborn's Challenge

One of the greatest soulwinners of this century has been Rev. T.L. Osborn of Tulsa, Oklahoma. Often, as he ministered in foreign countries, he was challenged by witch doctors and pagan priests who believed that their gods were greater than his. He would answer them, "Bring here a person who is known to be totally deaf. I will give you an opportunity to pray first in the name of your god. If your god opens his ears, then we will serve your god; but if my God opens his ears, we will serve mine."

Many times–not once or twice, but many times–

Such As I Have

Tommy Osborn's God unstopped those ears and those people who witnessed the miracle were turned unto the true and living God. There is power in that name. Praise God! And we are serving that same miracle-working God.

Luke Moody Reppy

In 1970 three of us were traveling in ministry in Indonesia. A young man named Luke Moody Reppy was our interpreter. He was a ball of fire for God. When he graduated from Bible School, he went to the Island of Borneo, where there were many devil worshipers, and began to preach the Gospel. He had to use an interpreter himself because he didn't know the local dialect.

Upon arriving at a certain village, he tried to witness for Christ. Both the tribal chief and the local witch doctor got upset. They decided to poison him.

The poison they put in the water was a type that causes your intestines to bleed, and before long you are dead. Brother Reppy drank all the water that was offered to him. His interpreter, however, was suspicious and didn't drink much of his.

The tribal leaders were so sure Luke Reppy would die that they started beating the drums in a way that signals that someone is either dead or dying. Sure enough, soon he began to pass blood. He took his interpreter and went out to the bank of the river. He said to his interpreter, "If I die, I want you to plant a cross here to let everyone know that a Christian has been here—one who wholly believed in the name of Jesus." Then he started to pray.

"Jesus," he said, "You said that if I drink any deadly thing, it would not hurt me (Mark 16:18). If You want to take me home for Your glory I am ready to go; but if You want to give me a little longer to serve You, I claim victory over this poison and I receive healing in the name of Jesus." Within moments after he began to call upon the name of Jesus, he felt the blood stop.

He could hear the sound of the drums announcing that someone had died; but he surely wasn't dead. He walked back into the village. All the villagers had gathered because of the drums. As he walked into the village, everyone just stood staring in disbelief. He walked right up to the chief and stared right back at him. The chief remained defiant. He still expected Brother Reppy to fall down at any moment. Minutes passed, and he didn't fall. Finally, his anointed gaze unnerved the chief, who broke down and began to weep. The entire village came to God that day. The name of Jesus is powerful!

That's a true story. I worked with the man. While

Such As I Have

I was in Indonesia, the wife of Luke Reppy gave birth to a son. God spoke to me to pay the hospital bill. They named the child Luke Wallace Reppy.

Faith In God = Faith Out of Everything Else

Our God is a miracle worker, and unknown saints throughout the world are standing for God and using the power that is in His precious name. If you can take your faith out of everything else and put it in the name of Jesus, you will have victory. You may find yourself ministering in Israel. You may find yourself ministering in China. You may find yourself ministering in England. You may find yourself ministering in Egypt. God will open for you the nations of the world–when you believe. Have faith in Him, *"faith in His Name!"*

Do not waiver! Do not falter! Let your faith be strong! Know that what the Scriptures promise is true:

> *Now unto Him that is able to do exceeding abundantly above all that we ask or think, according to the power that worketh in us, Unto Him be glory in the church by Christ Jesus throughout all ages world without end. Amen.*　　　　　　　　Ephesians 3:20-21

He can do *"exceeding abundantly above all that we ask or think."*

Sometimes folks get discouraged just before the miracle is about to take place. Because they have lost faith that it will happen, God cannot perform the miracle. But when our faith is sure and we are standing upon the rock of Christ Jesus, He will be right there. Let your faith be released. Allow the Holy Ghost to make you know:

> *God is not a man, that He should lie.*
> Numbers 23:19

The Word that our God has spoken He will fulfill.

My First Visit To the Holy Land

In 1963 Kash Amburgy called my father to say, "We have just formed a company for taking people to the Holy Land. I think you and your son should go."

My dad got off the telephone and told what had been said. I didn't have a dime, yet something hit me right in the pit of the stomach, and I said, "I'm going." The cost then was $1,495.00. I had no idea how I was going to get $1,495.00. But something within me said, "You are going!"

Such As I Have

In the days that followed, the devil repeatedly tried to discourage me and make me feel that going to the Holy Land was an impossibility for me. I hadn't worked at a secular job in months and didn't have a check coming in.

I began to believe, to trust God, to learn lessons of faith. I got sandpapered by the Holy Ghost; and when the Holy Ghost took a rest, Mother and Dad and Ruth took over. When one of them rested, others were busy working me over with good old-fashioned sand paper of the coarsest variety. They kept encouraging me to believe and grow in God. Something within me kept saying, "I'm going! I'm going! I'm going! I'm going!"

I went. When I got on the plane, I had $35.00 to my name. I saw other people spending hundreds of dollars on souvenirs and I couldn't. But no one had a better time than I had. I shouted the victory. While they were out buying souvenirs–Alexandrite stone, native dresses, wooden Camels and other Holy Land trinkets–I took a few folks with me and went back to the empty tomb. I stretched out in that empty tomb where Jesus had lain; and I had myself a time. Hallelujah!

I can testify to you that He is not there. The tomb is empty. He is alive! Hold on to the promise God has given you. It is sure! If He told you that your husband will get saved, don't let that Word fall to the ground. If He said your mother or father will get saved, don't let that promise fall to the ground. They may go out and commit worse sins and get "meaner" and madder than they have ever been, but cling to the promise of God. Put your faith in Him!

His Faith

The Apostle Paul wrote:

> *I am crucified with Christ: nevertheless, I live; yet not I, but Christ liveth in me: and the life which I now live in the flesh I live by THE FAITH OF THE SON OF GOD, who loved me, and gave Himself for me.*
>
> Galatians 2:20

It is not your faith. Your faith is weak. It is HIS faith. With HIS faith you will make it. It's HIS faith. We are going to make it! We are going to make it! We are going to make it! We are going to make it! Why? Because our faith is in HIM, not in men.

Every time you put your confidence in man, man will fail you. Believe me. It is true. If someone were to give you a dollar every Wednesday night for the next two months, you would begin to expect it. But when you got to the place you were expecting that dollar, it wouldn't come. You would cause it to fail

Such As I Have

by looking to man. When you *"look ... unto Jesus, the Author and Finisher of [y]our faith,"* you will receive the release that only Jesus can give. Praise His Name!

He will make a way where there seems to be no way. Put your hand in the nail-scarred hands. Feel the security that only Jesus can give.

What happened as the result of Peter's preaching? He must have preached a very good sermon. The Bible says that five thousand souls were added to the Church. Why? It was because Peter preached faith, not in himself and John, but in Jesus.

Jesus said:

> *And I, if I be lifted up ... will draw all men unto Me.* John 12:32

It is still true today. We are serving a God that is alive, and is moving and working mightily by His Spirit.

Take your eyes off your bank account. Take your eyes off your savings account–what you may have there or what you may not. Take your eyes off natural resources, and look unto Jesus. Know that as the Lord has spoken it in your ear, there will be a performance.

We're not weak. Just as faith in His name made that lame man strong, we are strong.

Do you feel that you are weak? The Scriptures say:

> *Let the weak say, 'I am strong.'*   Joel 3:10

You are strong.

Peter continued his message:

> *The faith which is by Him hath given him this perfect soundness in the presence of you all.*
> Acts 3:16

Many folks don't understand how we can stand in the midst of the storm and be strong in God. They don't understand. When everybody else seems to be in a tizzy, and are "all shook up" because of the natural tragedies happening all around them, we can stand with such peace and such confidence. It is because our faith is in Jesus. Amen! It is because He has made us strong. If we do not waiver, but keep our eyes upon Him, He cannot fail to grant us the promise He has made. Don't allow an element of doubt to come in.

I have heard people say, "I don't understand why it didn't come to pass. I had great faith." No they didn't. If you have faith, that faith produces the necessary miracle. Faith is spiritual. Faith is a gift. Faith is a fruit of the Spirit. As we let our faith be released, we will see the fulfillment of the promise that God has spoken to us.

Poor–and Do I Mean Poor

I don't know any family here in America that was any poorer than our family. We were poor, not only when I was a boy. We were still poor in 1962 and 1963 after I was first saved. And when I say poor, I mean POOR. Because we never had anything, however, we couldn't depend on what we had. I thank God for that. I thank Him for every lesson of faith I was taught.

I thank God for Christmastime when I was a child. My mother and father didn't tell me that Santa Clause was coming down the chimney. They said, "If you want something, you must pray and ask God for it."

My sister and I would open the Sears & Roebuck Catalog or the Western Auto Toy Book, circle what we wanted–with the size and the color we wanted–and then just ask Jesus for it. Nobody ever knew what we had circled–except Jesus.

When Christmas day arrived, the exact fire engine that I had wanted came from one side of town. The exact doll baby and the exact carriage Ruth had wanted came from the other side of town. We always got what we had requested from the Lord because He spoke to somebody on one side of town to bring that exact model number and spoke to somebody else on the other side to bring exactly what Ruth wanted. That is the way we were taught.

When Dad died in 1972, he didn't leave us anything–speaking of this world's goods, but he left us two things that money could not buy: liberty of the Spirit and faith in God.

Thank God for every time we didn't have a bed to sleep in, every time we had holes in our shoes, every time there wasn't enough food on the table. Thank God for every time the house was cold because there wasn't enough money to heat it correctly. I say "Thank God" because these experiences made us know that our God can pull us through, whatever the circumstances.

There is nothing impossible with God! We can stand upon His assurance and know that when He has spoken, He will fulfill His Word. Your dream will be fulfilled when you begin to say, "Such as I have. Such as I have."

Say, "I am going to the Holy Land with SUCH AS I HAVE," "I am going to India to minister for God with SUCH AS I HAVE." If you are willing to believe Him, God will take "SUCH AS [YOU] HAVE" and cause it to grow and multiply until every need is met.

Thank God we are not a people that wait until it

is all in our hand before we ever get ready. We start with "SUCH AS [WE] HAVE" and believe God to supply what is lacking.

Five Pieces of Bread and Two Small Fish

In the story of the little boy who had the five barley loaves and two small fish, Philip asked:

What are they among so many?   John 6:9

It seemed like a legitimate question, but when Jesus used "SUCH AS [THE BOY] HAD," it was multiplied until it fed a multitude.

"SUCH AS [YOU AND] I HAVE" is sufficient to meet the needs of people all over the world. That's why God is trying to get us out where the needs are and make us realize that He is the miracle-working God. He will use what we have to perform miracles for the benefit of the those in need.

Such As They Had Stirred India

In November of 1978, we were late in arriving for our scheduled meetings in Ahmedabad, India because we got stranded in the turmoil of the deteriorating situation in Teheran. We finally arrived in

Power In Your Hand

India on what should have been the last night of the meeting. There were about two hundred people present. I preached that night. Afterward, I did not feel that the meeting should close, although many of us were scheduled to go on to other places. I asked some of the others who were with us if they would be willing to stay and continue the meeting.

The first person I asked answered, "No."

One young brother from the Midwest said, "My wife and I would like to stay."

A young sister from North Carolina said, "Brother Heflin, I'd like to stay too."

So, those three stayed on in Ahmedabad to continue the meeting. The three of them were young in the Lord and together didn't have much to offer, but "SUCH AS [THEY HAD]" they were ready to give. No mission board would have sent them out, but "SUCH AS [THEY HAD]" they were willing to impart to others.

We were gone for three or four days. When we came back, the meeting had grown from a couple of hundred to nearly a thousand. I went out for three or four more days and by the time I got back, there were nearly two thousand, five hundred people attending the meeting.

What had happened? That young brother started giving out what he had, and the Holy Ghost started multiplying it. His wife started giving out what she

Such As I Have

had, and the Lord multiplied it. That "Tarheel" started giving out what she had, and the Lord multiplied it.

A man had been hit by a car. His legs and arms were broken. They prayed for him one afternoon. God healed him, and the crowd automatically doubled. The place was shaken by the power of God. When I got back there, I saw that they had roped off the front of the meeting area. I asked why.

"Brother Heflin," they told me, "you will never believe it. We had a fist fight last night in church."

I said, "You had what? In church?"

"The people wanted to get prayed for so badly because miracles were taking place that they began fighting over who was going to be first in line."

"What did you do?" I asked.

"We got the biggest Indian we could find and put him over the healing line."

Why did it happen? They were giving "SUCH AS [THEY HAD]" and the Holy Ghost used it. It grew and grew and grew and grew some more, until it was sufficient to meet the need of the hour. And that which is in you will grow in the same way. We are going to give "SUCH AS [WE] HAVE" to the lost and dying world, and Jesus will come and put His hand of multiplication upon it. God will do the work.

God is looking for somebody willing to give. Are you willing to give? Are you willing to give of yourself? Are you willing to use the little bit that you have?

How Do You Know You Can't Do It Already?

The lying devil will tell you that what you have is not enough. The Scriptures assure us:

He is a liar and the father of it.   John 8:44

Satan causes you to look at someone else and think, "If I only had what they have, I would be okay." How do you know you don't have more than they have? You will never know until you get busy and start using it.

When I first got saved I was doing a lot of fasting. One day my dad came to me in the kitchen. He said, "Son, what are you fasting for?"

I answered, "Dad, I want to pray for the sick. I want to pray for the blind, that they might see, and the lame, that they might run and leap for joy."

He said, "That's wonderful!" Then he looked around the kitchen for a moment and said, "I don't see any blind people here. I don't see any crippled here. How do you know God hasn't already given you what you are praying for?"

Such As I Have

He was right. You will never know until you find somebody in need and you lay your hand on them and realize that you are stronger and that "SUCH AS [YOU] HAVE" can make somebody else strong as well.

The Holy Ghost will do the same thing for you that He did for the lame man. The Holy Ghost made that man stand on his feet; and the Holy Ghost made you and me stand up — not in our own strength or power, but in the power and the anointing of the Spirit. We can say, "SUCH AS I HAVE GIVE I UNTO THEE."

Whether you believe this or not is very important:

As (a man) thinketh in his heart, so is he.
Proverbs 23:7

If the devil tells you that you have no power and you believe him, you will be powerless. But when you believe that the authority and power of God has been invested in you (as the Word of God teaches), you will see the mighty miracles that God has promised to you.

God wants to place a fresh anointing upon your hands right now. Receive it and let God multiply the little you already have.

Part Three:
A Man Sent By God

Who Was the Man God Sent?

There was a man sent from God, whose name was John. John 1:6

Take out "John" and put your own name there.

"There was a man sent from God, whose name was [Wallace Heflin]."

"There was a woman sent from God, whose name was [Edith Heflin]."

Put your name in that spot. That's YOU. YOU are the one that God wants to send.

Often we consider the great things that God has done for somebody else and yet allow the devil to minimize what God has given to us personally. I want to challenge YOU to stir up that which is lying dormant within YOU. I want YOU to realize that God has called YOU, chosen YOU, and is willing to send YOU.

A special anointing comes upon those who are sent. That special anointing is not for the purpose of telling our own story. It is not to "do our own thing." It is not to build up a reputation for ourselves. It is not to put our name up in lights. It is not so that people might see us, that we might be deified in the eyes of man, that we might win popularity contests, or that our name might be flashed across America and become a household word.

God sends us to be His mouthpiece, to deliver His Word, to stand with His authority and say, "Thus saith the Lord." That places a great responsibility on us.

Apologizing For God

Never apologize for the message God gives you to deliver. You don't have to defend the Word of God.

Many years ago a spirit-filled, Methodist preacher came to our town, stayed in our house and attended a ministerial meeting with my father and me. In that meeting there were two denominational ministers who had graduated from a large, well known divinity school. When they graduated, they believed in nothing. After the ministerial meeting was over, they began to argue about the supernatural and the miraculous.

My feathers got ruffled and I began to tell them, in no uncertain terms, that the Word of God was true. I was very proud of how I handled myself in that argument.

A Man Sent By God

When we got home, however, that good, spirit-filled Methodist brother said to me, "Brother Heflin, I was a little disappointed in you today."

My feathers began to fall a little bit.

"I was disappointed," he continued, "that you were trying to defend the Word of God. The Word of God needs no defense."

He was right. You and I don't need to defend the Word of God. Despite what men say, the Word of God is true. The Bible says:

Let God be true, but every man a liar.
Romans 3:4

When you are delivering the message that the Holy Ghost has given you to deliver, you don't have to apologize. You don't have to defend the Word of God. It is *"yea and amen."*

One of My First Revivals

Just a couple of years after I got saved, my father asked me to preach a week's revival in our church. It was one of the first revivals I held. The meeting was blessed and went on for four weeks. One night I began to preach from the Scripture that says:

Power In Your Hand

And He gave them their request; but sent leanness into their soul.   Psalm 106:15

In the course of the message I stated that long hair is a woman's glory and that women were doing themselves a spiritual disservice by ignoring that truth. The ladies forgot everything I had preached during the first twenty-seven nights; but they sure remembered that message.

After the service a woman came to me and said, "Brother Heflin, you made (so and so) cry."

I said, "Was it something I said that made her cry? Or was it the Word of God? I cannot apologize for what the Word of God says. If it was something that I said that offended her, I will be the first to apologize. But I cannot apologize for what the Word of God says."

My friend, believe the Scriptures:

For the prophecy came not in old time by the will of man: but holy men of God spake as they were moved by the Holy Ghost.   2 Peter 1:21

When God calls you to preach and sends you to deliver a message, you must not budge from the message. You have no authority and no right to alter the message that God has given you. You must declare it exactly as God gives it to you and you must be willing to stand behind the message.

A Man Sent By God

We do not stand in our own power nor in our own authority. We stand representing Heaven. While Jesus was here He said:

> *All power is given unto me in Heaven and in earth. Go ye therefore.*   Matthew 28:18-19

We stand in the authority and power of Heaven. And when we speak the Word, Heaven will move to confirm it.

An Eleven-Thousand-Dollar Miracle

We laid hands on a woman at the end of one of the campmeeting services in the sixties. She needed a great miracle in her business. She said to me, "Brother Heflin, there is no need for me to go to work tomorrow unless God gives me ten thousand dollars. I want you to pray and agree with me that it will be there. In the natural it is an impossibility."

As I laid hands on her, the Spirit of God began to say, "It is but a light thing."

My flesh said, "What in the world am I saying?" It was ten thirty at night and she needed ten thousand dollars by the next morning. That was certainly not a "light thing." But I was not speaking as Wallace Heflin. I was speaking as the voice of God.

The Holy Ghost said, "It is but a light thing. By the time you get all the pieces together, you will not understand how it has been done; but it shall be so."

The next morning, when the woman arrived at her place of business, she found that God had kept His Word. More than eleven thousand dollars had come in. What I had given her was a message from God, and He brought it to pass because He never fails.

A Call To Nigeria

I laid hands on a sister from Cleveland while she was at camp that same summer and God also gave her a word of prophecy. The Lord said, "You will travel; and you will travel as you have never traveled before." While ministering to her I saw a multitude of people. The Lord said to her, "You will not just call out one condition and have one person healed. You will call out one condition, and there will be seven or twelve or twenty with that same condition that will stand throughout that mass of people and declare that they have been healed."

She came to me a day or so later and asked, "Do you know where that crowd of people was? I've been on the phone talking to my husband. He is in

A Man Sent By God

New York talking to a senator from Nigeria. We have been invited to go there and conduct a campaign in March."

My friend, when the Holy Ghost speaks, you can stand on what He has spoken. It will surely come to pass. We do not speak of ourselves. When you and I are called and chosen and sent, Heaven is standing behind us and the Word of God will be fulfilled.

Just be willing to give yourself wholly to God so that nothing can hinder the flow of the Holy Ghost.

Choosing the Recipient of Our Message

The Bible tells us of a stubborn and rebellious preacher named Jonah whom God had called and chosen and sent to deliver His message. Jonah was a Jew and didn't want to go and preach to the Gentiles of Nineveh. He knew that God wanted to save them.

I imagine him saying to God (because he didn't think these people deserved salvation), "I know that if I go down there and preach the Gospel, You will save them, and I don't want You to save them. Let them be lost!" In the end, however, he had to go, for one thing you and I cannot do is pick and choose to whom we will preach.

A great man of God came into Richmond many years ago to preach, but some local ministers rose up against him because he wanted to invite people of all races, and they wanted to remain segregated. He said to them, "When you stand before God, brethren, you will give an account of the souls you have hindered from getting into Heaven."

We cannot pick and choose whether we will preach to the rich or the poor, to the white or the black, to the Indian, to the African, to the Chinese. When the Holy Ghost sends you as a messenger, just be obedient to Him.

Jonah Had the Money He Needed

Jonah rebelled. He had the money, but he bought a ticket going the wrong way. He also had the time, but he chose to spend it running from God's will.

We say, "If I just had the money ... If I just had the time ... Oh, what I would do for God!" But when God gives us the money and gives us the time, we still rebel.

Jonah had the transportation.

"God, if I just had a new car ..." Or, "If You just give me an airline ticket, God ..." "If You just made a way, what I would do for You!"

Many years ago some church people had said to

us, "If I had a way to get to church, I would not miss a night." So we bought some buses to go after them. We painted those buses white and those white busses stopped in front of the houses of those "If-Only" people every Wednesday night, Friday night and Sunday night. But they made liars out of so many people. They were not planning to go to church. They were just making excuses.

We have the money.

We have the time.

We have the transportation.

Let us be the people sent by God.

Jonah Had the Message

Jonah had the message but didn't want to deliver it. He didn't want to be obedient. After he was thrown overboard and was swallowed by the whale, however, he started to change his attitude. He said:

> *I cried by reason of mine affliction unto the LORD, ... out of the belly of hell cried I.*
>
> Jonah 2:2

> *The waters compassed me about, even to the soul: the depth closed me round about, the weeds were wrapped about my head.*
>
> Jonah 2:5

Power In Your Hand

When God got finished with the prophet he was ready to go to Nineveh.

We have the message. God has given it to us. The message is "Jesus is coming soon." We don't need a homiletical outline. We don't need to have A, B, C, D and E. We don't absolutely have to have points 1, 2 and 3. We have a starting point, and that is to tell them that Jesus died, rose again, is coming soon, and they should be ready.

God is looking for men and women He can send to do the job in these last days and who won't run the other way. When the old whale spit Jonah out, he hit the beach running. He was ready.

It is not necessary for so many troubles to come our way and for so much of the judgment of God to be poured forth upon us. God wants us to move in obedience to Him before the difficulties come. The Bible says:

> *The gifts and calling of God are without repentance.*   Romans 11:29

Since God has put His hand upon you and upon me we are no longer our own. We belong to Him.

Jonah preached with great fervor. He had the greatest revival the Bible records. One hundred and twenty thousand people didn't know their right hand from the left, but they had revival. Why?

A Man Sent By God

Because Jonah had gone through the judgments of God.

Jonah had an eight word sermon:

> *Yet forty days, and Nineveh shall be overthrown.*   Jonah 3:4

Jonah preached with such fire and such fervor that even the king heard the message and called a time of fasting and prayer. When you preach as a man or woman from another world, people will listen. The devil will know that you are present. And God will confirm the Word with signs and wonders and miracles.

The devil isn't happy about someone preaching hell, fire and brimstone. The devil doesn't want someone preaching a separated, consecrated life. He doesn't want someone to preach about a life of holiness, a life of separation, a life of godliness.

It doesn't matter, however, what he wants. When we stand in God's power and holiness and declare His message, God will always back us up. When we stand and deliver the message that God has given us, miracles happen and the blessings of God are rich upon us.

Philip Preached Christ

Philip was one of those that waited on tables in

Power In Your Hand

the early church. But he stayed full of wisdom, full of faith, and full of the Holy Ghost. One day God said, "That's enough Philip. You have cleaned tables long enough. You have ministered to those widows long enough. I am going to chase you out to greener pastures now." God sent him to Samaria, and there he brought Holy Ghost revival.

There is no record of Philip having ever stood and preached a sermon before that time, but when God sent him to Samaria, the Bible relates that he preached Christ and the city was stirred:

> *And there was great joy in that city.*
> Acts 8:8

Philip didn't preach his organization. He didn't preach pet doctrines and theories and ideas. He preached Christ. Jesus said:

> *And I, if I be lifted up ... will draw all men unto Me.*
> John 12:32

Samaria was shaken because Philip had been sent to do a work for God.

Then, right in the midst of the great revival, God said, "I have another job for you. You have handled this so wonderfully. You have been obedient. You have done exactly what I told you to do. The city is stirred because you preached the Word

A Man Sent By God

that I gave you. Now, I have another special assignment. I have a man, one man, one man to whom I want to send you."

If that would happen today, I can imagine what some of our preachers would say. "God, don't you know I am a city-wide evangelist. I am an auditorium man. I am a big stadium man. I am a big TV personality. Surely You're not going to send me to talk to just one person. Oh God, can't You find someone else that You haven't used as greatly as You have used me? Can't You send them to do this job?"

Thank God that Philip was just as zealous to go to the one as he was to go to the city crowd. My friend, if God sends you out of your way to minister to one soul, be faithful to give that person the same measure of the Gospel that you have received from others. You never know what that seed might bring forth.

Because Philip preached to the Ethiopian eunuch and he, in turn, took the message home, Ethiopia has been a Christian country in the midst of all the Moslem nations of Africa. You never know what one seed will produce for God.

The Largest Church in the New Hebrides

Another minister and I were in Australia in 1975, and we left there a few days before New Year's

Day. Two of our camp ladies had already flown to the New Hebrides Islands in the Pacific. We went to the Fiji islands and spent New Year's there, waiting for them to finish what God had sent them to do, then meet us, so we could fly home together.

When they arrived at Fiji they were very ecxited. "You will never believe who we ran into," they told us. "The man who is pastoring the largest church in the New Hebrides. He has between five hundred and seven hundred members. He says that he got saved under your ministry in 1970. He said, 'Tell Brother Heflin that I am going on for God.' "

I didn't remember that brother. I just sowed the seeds. We sometimes never know what happens later. Just give of yourselves and allow the Spirit of God to challenge men and women. As you are faithful, God will do the work.

God is looking for men and women that He can send. Are you a candidate?

The Runner Who Had No Message

The Bible tells a story of two messengers: Joab, David's general, wanted to send a message to the king that although the battle had gone well, his son, Absalom, had been killed. He called a runner named Cushi and commissioned him to run with the message (2 Samuel 18:21).

A Man Sent By God

Just then another runner, Ahimaaz, came and said to Joab:

Let me, I pray thee also run. 2 Samuel 18:22

Joab's answer was:

Wherefore wilt thou run, my son, seeing that thou hast no tidings ready? Same verse

This man didn't know all the facts. He hadn't seen the death of Absalom. His message was incomplete.

The young man insisted:

Let me run. Verse 23

Finally, Joab consented. "*Run,*" he told him.

The second runner outran the first. A watchman that David had sent to the top of the wall spotted the runner coming. He recognized him and gave the word to David who knew Ahimaaz as a good man who surely brought a good message.

Then, the other runner was spotted, and everyone waited in anticipation of the message each would bring.

When Ahimaaz arrived, however, and fell before

the king, he could only say what he knew: that their enemies were defeated. When David asked about the fate of Absalom, the runner had to answer:

> *I saw a great tumult, but I knew not what it was.* Verse 29

David told Ahimaaz to stand aside and make room for the messenger who was commissioned and who had the message. Thus, the sad news reached the ears of the king.

There are so many today just "in it" for the run. They just want to run. They don't have anything to say, and after they get where they are going, they have nothing to give. They just want to go so that when they come home, they can tell someone they went.

When I was in India in 1978 some foreigners were there ministering. I guess I shouldn't say ministering. They were living in India. They had no message to give. They were actually a reproach to the Gospel. Everyone back home thought they were doing some great work for God.

People who give need to exercise discernment about their giving and to not give because of every sob story they hear. Let us finance the anointing.

A Man Sent By God

Find someone who is doing something for God and stand behind them.

We are not responsible to promote those who are building a kingdom for themselves. Find those who have God's message. It is not enough to deliver what *we think*.

It is not enough just to run and those who only run will someday be idled by difficulty. If trouble comes throughout the world, it won't stop those being sent of God. The called and chosen will not miss one airplane ticket. They will not miss one engagement. But trouble will keep home many people that are sending themselves. Why? Because God will not supply the need. God will always provide for those whom He has called and chosen and sent. He will always make a way. And His hand is upon YOU!

Don't worry about finances. Get your soul anointed with the Holy Ghost and God will provide your financial needs. As you go to deliver the message, He will confirm the Word, and great shall be the report of that which the Holy Ghost has done.

Thank God He is raising up "nobodies" in these days, those whom no one else has heard of before. The hour is late! The time is short! And while there is still time, you and I must get busy doing God's bidding.

Power In Your Hand

Jesus Did His Father's Will

Jesus said:

> *My meat is to do the will of Him that sent Me, and to finish HIS WORK.* John 4:34

He repeated the same thing in various ways in other parts of John:

> *I seek not mine own will, but THE WILL OF THE FATHER which hath sent Me.* 5:30

> *For I came down from heaven, not to do mine own will, but THE WILL OF HIM THAT SENT ME.* 6:38

> *I must work THE WORKS OF HIM that sent Me.* 9:4

God wants you and I to move into that same place, that we no longer do our own will but the will of the One who has sent us.

God might send you to your neighbor. That is just as important as going to China. God might send you to someone on your job. That is just as important as going overseas. The message that God gives you to deliver to the one that is across the street is just as important as a message taken to a king or a ruler. It is God's message. It is God's appointed hour.

Isaiah said:

> *The Lord God hath given me the tongue of the learned, that I should know how to speak a word in season to him that is weary.*
> Isaiah 50:4

May we, with the authority and the power of the Holy Ghost, deliver to them the Word and may we look at them and say, "Thus saith the Lord." And when we say, "Thus saith the Lord," He will be there.

When we lay hands on the sick, we are not doing it for some selfish desire. We are fulfilling the commission that God has given to us:

> *They shall lay hands on the sick, and they shall recover.*
> Mark 16:18

Laying hands on the sick is just being obedient to the One Who has sent us.

Not Always Pleasant

The message that God gives us is not always a pleasant one. Did you ever have to deliver a message that wasn't so sweet, one that you really hated to deliver, one that you wished somebody else was chosen to give? You said, "Lord, couldn't you raise up somebody else that could do it? Do I have to say it? Do I have to declare it? Do I have to reveal it? Are you sure, God, there is no way for me to get out of this?"

It is not always easy to deliver God's message, but when He gives you a message, stand and declare it. Say, "This is what the Lord has shown me. This is what the Lord revealed to me. This is what God has given me."

Nathan the prophet was raised up to go and speak to King David when he had sinned with Bathsheba. I am sure that Nathan must have been trembling at the thought, but he knew that God had given him the message to deliver; and he had to be faithful with the message.

A lovely message may be easy to deliver. If it is wonderful and sweet, that may be easier. You know it will be well received, even appreciated. So it is no problem for you to go. Your flesh even wants to do it. When the message, however, is something that is not convenient, not easy to give, our flesh rebels.

Ananias Rebelled

In Bible days, a man by the name of Ananias was

A Man Sent By God

praying. He said, "Oh, God, use me. Send me. Let me be a faithful servant, a witness and a messenger."

God answered him, "*I will*" and gave him a specific assignment:

> *Arise, and go into the street which is called Straight, and enquire in the house of Judas for one called Saul.*   Acts 9:11

God had a message for Saul and he chose Ananias to deliver it, but Ananias was not so enthusiastic once he knew that it involved the hated Saul. "Oh! No! Lord," he cried, "not him! That man has letters of authority in his pocket to kill people like me!" This was something that Ananias' flesh did not want to do.

But God said, "Go!" And when God told him to go, it was because He had prepared Saul. God said to Ananias, "Don't worry about Saul. I have already blinded him. He can't see you. Anyway, I have him on his knees. He is praying."

That's different, isn't it? Whatever the task God calls you to do, He has already prepared the way. He is trying to loose you from the entanglements, the bondages. Friends, we have set still long enough. We have made excuses long enough. It is time to stir ourselves. Don't make any more excuses! Offer yourself to God. Say, "God, I am a candidate to be your messenger. I want you to send me." Then, watch out! God will confirm His Word. You will never know until you speak. You will never know until you go.

Be that man or woman sent by God.

An Exodus From the Camp

During camptime in 1979 God told us there would be a great exodus from camp, that more of our people would go to the nations of the world than ever before. Some folks went home to sell things and head overseas for God. God put His hand on many that year. And each year He has done the same. It has not been unusual for twenty-five to forty to be out in many nations traveling and bringing the Good News because of God's dealings with us during the camptime. He is still looking for those He can send.

Don't be one of those who says:

"Lord, I am not able."
"I am not old enough."
"I am too old."
"I am not capable."
"I am not well educated."
"I don't have the money."

Stop making excuses and just say, "God, here I am. If You want me to go, I am ready. If you want to send me, I'm ready."

The Messengers God Chooses

Frequently half of the joy is seeing the messenger that God uses to deliver His Word. He never picks those who are the "logical choices." He never chooses according to our criteria. He selects some of the most unusual people to do His work. It blesses your heart to know they have been faithful to that which the Spirit of God has called them.

God's raising up men and women to stand, to stand with strong and straight backs, to look the devil in the eye and not compromise an inch. If you are a compromiser, it is better not to offer yourself to God. He is looking for men and women that will not compromise. He is looking for those that will declare the Word and not change It.

My personal experience with having people perform some duty is interesting. You give some people instructions, you tell them exactly what to do, and they do just the opposite. They inject their own opinions, their own thoughts. They say, "I thought that was good; so I said it. I did it."

It is reported to me occasionally that someone says "Brother Heflin told me to do it," when, in reality, I never told them any such thing. I told them to do it another way, but they decided that their way was better.

We cannot do that with God. When you say, "God, I will tell it like it is, I will go exactly where You send me, I will be there at the appointed time," you must keep your word.

On New Year's Eve of 1978, I was in Elizabeth, South Australia. The Holy Ghost spoke to me and said the words "RIGHT ON TIME IN '79." It sounded like a cliché, but the Lord said to me, "If you will be where I want you at the appointed hour, I will be right where you want Me at the appointed hour." My friend, I have seen the Holy Ghost do some unusual and glorious things. Why? Because I was where God wanted me when He wanted me there.

When we say "Yes, Lord," He will thrust us forth quickly, and God's work will be done.

Walking By Revelation

There was a man sent from God, whose name was John.   John 1:6

John didn't understand all that he was doing. He was walking by revelation. God had spoken to him. There had been no prophets in the land for four

A Man Sent By God

hundred years. There was no case history or recent Bible record to refer to. There was no other ministry to pattern himself after.

All he knew was the One that called him to baptize in water said to him:

> *Upon Whom thou shalt see the Spirit descending, and remaining on Him, that same is He which baptizeth with the Holy Ghost.*
> John 1:33

During the entire ministry of John, he was looking for the One upon Whom the anointing would descend.

We cannot afford to pattern our ministries after somebody else. We cannot simply adopt the mannerisms or be a copycat of another minister. God has made you an individual. You are a handmade vessel.

The Bible says:

> *There are diversities of gifts, but the same Spirit. And there are differences of administrations, but the same Lord. And there are diversities of operations, but it is the same God which worketh all in all.* 1 Corinthians 12:4-6

The word of knowledge and prophecy can flow

differently out of you than it does from somebody else. Don't try to copy or imitate. Be yourself. Be the messenger that God wants you to be.

It is God's time to deliver the message. It is God's time to thrust us forth. If you will say "Lord, I am ready to be sent," He will send you.

Be that person that God can send.

Part Four:
Availability

The Problem

I beseech you therefore, brethren, by the mercies of God, that ye present your bodies a living sacrifice, holy, acceptable unto God, which is your reasonable service. And be not conformed to this world: but be ye transformed by the renewing of your mind, that ye may prove what is that good, and acceptable, and perfect, will of God.   Romans 12:1-2

It is time to make ourselves available to God. I am angry because too many of God's people are being tricked by the enemy. They are allowing things to happen in their lives which make them unavailable to the work of the ministry.

God wants us to be available! God wants us to be "Johnny on the spot." God wants us to be like an EVEREADY flashlight–just press the button and it's on. God wants us to keep ourselves in a position so that anytime, day or night, we can be ready to move as the Holy Ghost directs us.

For five years I accompanied my sister Ruth to

the airport each time she would leave for a mission trip abroad. She said to me, "Take good care of Mother. Take good care of Dad. Be a good boy until I get home."

She kissed me good-bye in the terminal. She went to the steps of the ramp. She looked back and waved good-bye to me. I watched her disappear into the interior of the plane. The plane took off and disappeared as well and I was left behind and had to drive home.

I prayed on my way home, saying, "Lord, I want to go too. I don't always want to be left at home. If You will just speak to me and tell me where You want me to go, I will get ready."

God answered that prayer. He showed me that Ruth was going while I was staying because Ruth knew the secret of availability. She kept herself ready, physically and spiritually. She kept a suitcase packed. She was available anytime, day or night. When the call of God came, she could pick up and go–sometimes with very short notice. She was available to do the will of God.

For example, during one summer campmeeting in the late sixties, God spoke to Ruth about ten or ten thirty one night to take a trip. Before midnight she had already booked the ticket and the next morning she caught the early plane. She didn't have the finances. But God moved on someone that

Availability

night to put the money in her hand. The next day she was on her way because she was available to do the will and purpose of God. Ruth has been to virtually every nation on the Earth, some of them many times, because of her obedience to the Lord.

You and I must make ourselves available to God and keep ourselves available at all times, so that when He calls we will be ready.

Perhaps Today

Many years ago God spoke to me to have a thousand lapel buttons made bearing the words "Perhaps Today!" He wanted me to arouse curiosity so that I could witness. The first curious person to ask me what the words meant was the woman in charge of production at the New Jersey company that made the buttons for me.

"I am curious," she wrote, "what does 'Perhaps Today!' mean? I think it refers to the Second Coming of the Lord. Please write and tell me if I'm right."

I wrote back and said, "I am so happy that you have been stirred. It is a sign to us that these buttons will be effective. I would like you to wear the first one."

Every time I wore one of those buttons on my lapel someone would ask me, "Perhaps Today! What does that mean?" Some people did curious things, even being impolite enough to lean across someone else in order to see what was on my lapel. "Perhaps Today."

One day I was in the Passport Office in the old Post Office Building in Richmond. The lady in charge of arranging passports saw the pin and asked, "Perhaps Today! What does that mean?" For the next twenty minutes, while I preached to her about the Second Coming of Jesus, the Lord did not allow another person to come in that door.

There were other times, however, that I had something else on my mind. When someone would say, "Perhaps Today! What does that mean?" I would say, "What? What did you say? Pardon me. I didn't hear what you said." I was caught off guard and did not have a ready answer and the opportunity was lost.

In those cases, I had to repent. I said, "God if You will forgive me, never again will I allow myself to be without a ready answer, without a clear reply. I want to be sharp for You. I want to be 'on the job' for You so that I may be able to effectively witness: 'Perhaps today you will get healed. Perhaps today your husband will get saved. Perhaps today Jesus might come. Perhaps today that financial miracle you need will come.' "

Availability

The buttons served to stir curiosity; but they helped me too. As long as I wore that button it reminded me to be available to be the witness that God wanted me to be.

You and I must make ourselves available to God to do His will and His bidding. When we are available, we will find new doors opening to us.

God might have called another to fill a certain position; but they were not available. They have, somehow, made themselves unavailable. So the Lord will raise you up or raise me up to get that job done.

What was Paul saying to the Romans? He was saying, "I want you to live a life that makes you available to do My bidding." That places on us the responsibility to be always ready.

Ready At All Times

Some folks don't think I give preachers enough advance warning before they are going to preach in our church and camp. I feel that we should be ready at all times. The anointing that is in us should be sufficient to get the job done. When we say, "Yes, God, I will keep myself available," God works.

I have invited preachers to come hold revival

meetings on short notice. Some have answered that it would take them a few weeks of fasting and prayer to get ready for revival. I don't even want them to come if it's going to take them weeks to get prayed through. I want someone that's already prayed through. And I certainly don't want to have to get them prayed through after they get here. I want somebody that is already prayed through, someone that keeps themselves in a position that the anointing of God can continually flow through their lives.

It is interesting. When some preachers hold revival meetings they fast and pray and get themselves in a place of anointing. After the revival is over, however, many of them slack up and drift back into the state they were in before. God is requiring more of us. He wants us to stay on the mountain top at all times so that the anointing of the Spirit can flow through us and into someone else.

You never know when you will be called on to give an account of your experience in God. You never know when you will be asked to speak or testify. You never know when YOU might need to lay YOUR hands on someone that is dying. You might come upon an accident. Someone's life might depend on YOUR prayer and YOUR faith.

Paul is saying to us in Romans 12:1-2, "Put yourselves upon the altar. Keep yourselves available to God." If you are available to God at all times you will be able to do His perfect will. If you are unavailable you cannot flow in what God wants of you.

The Unwanted Hair Cut

Many years ago one of our brothers came back from ministering overseas. He was told by one of the ladies in charge that he needed a hair cut. He got upset and said, "I don't need any woman telling me what to do."

Eventually, someone was called to cut his hair. He didn't like the way it was cut; so, he shaved his head. By the time he felt shame for his terrible attitude and his rebellious spirit, it was too late. I saw him wearing a farmer's hat with a big, wide brim. I watched him for several days. He would pull that hat way down on his head to hide his baldness. I didn't say a word. I purposely stayed out of his way–until I noticed that another young man had shaved his head too.

I said, "That's enough." I cornered the first one in the kitchen. I said, "What in the world have you done?"

He said, "I am a man. I don't need a woman telling me what to do."

Power In Your Hand

I said, "You're acting like a child, and somebody does need to tell you what to do."

"I'm thirty-five years old, and I guess I know what is right," he replied.

I said, "You don't act like you know what is right. Do you realize what you have done? You flew in from overseas to be here at campmeeting time. But by this act of rebellion, you made yourself unavailable to God. All you need is a saffron robe and some sandals, and everyone will think that you are a Buddhist monk. Who wants you to lay your hands on them? Nobody wants you to touch them. Nobody wants to be around you. You have already put yourself on a shelf. You are unavailable to do what God sent you home to do." Too late that brother realized how the devil had tricked him.

Paul said:

> *I keep under my body, and bring it into subjection: lest that by any means, when I have preached to others, I myself should be a castaway.* 1 Corinthians 9:27

A castaway is something or someone that no longer is used. Something else or someone else is used instead.

That is exactly what happened to the young man I am telling you about. I felt sorry for him. He

Availability

seemed to be genuinely repentant. He recognized that he had made a mistake. A great compassion came over me, and I began to pray for him. I prayed for God to take away the reproach and cause his hair to grow, to move swiftly to restore him to a place of usefulness and service to God.

You should have seen his hair grow. His wife came to me later and said, "I don't know what you did, but I wish you hadn't prayed quite so hard. My husband has the fullest head of hair I have ever seen." To this day she tells me, "I wish you hadn't prayed quite so hard." God answered prayer and made that man once more available to do what God had called him to do.

Keep yourself in that place of service to God.

Knowing the Will of God

Paul challenged the Romans:

> *I beseech you therefore, brethren, by the mercies of God, that ye present your bodies a living sacrifice, holy, acceptable unto God, which is your reasonable service. And be not conformed to this world: but be ye transformed by the renewing of your mind, that ye may prove*

Power In Your Hand

what is that good, and acceptable, and perfect, will of God.   Romans 12:1-2

If you want to know what God's perfect will is, then make yourself available to Him. He will make you know His perfect will.

I want to be more available to God than I have ever been. If God says in the middle of the night, "I want you to rise and go," I want to go. If, while I am getting a few hours of rest, God wants to carry my spirit out to another country, into a prison camp, to somewhere in Israel, or China or Russia, I want to be available to God.

If God wants to pick you up in the daytime and physically transport you to some other place, be available. Be open to the Spirit of God. Keep your affairs in such order that in a moment's time you could pick up a suitcase and travel for the glory of the Lord Jesus Christ.

Mother will soon be seventy-eight. I can guarantee you that within thirty minutes she could be ready to leave her house and catch a flight to wherever God might send her. She keeps a small suitcase packed. She keeps her toothpaste, her toothbrush, some bobby pins, her brush and a few other necessities in that little case. She can just pick it up and go. You need to be available too.

Availability

We need to stay in a place of communion with God, with our ear attuned to hear His still, small voice. We need to be in a position that God can wake us up in the middle of the night and let us know that a missionary on some mission field is in danger. Our prayers must deliver them and see them through.

"Sleep in the Bathtub"

Some years ago God spoke to a sister in Jerusalem to get out of bed and go sleep in the bathtub. How many of you would have done such a foolish thing? It was one or one thirty in the morning. God said, "Get out of bed, and sleep in the bathtub."

She had heard God's voice before, so she grabbed some bed clothes, went to the bathroom, and got in the bathtub. Moments later a hand reached in the window by her bed to grab her.

In Haifa, fifty or sixty miles away, God spoke to another couple at the same hour, waking them up as well, and said, "Pray for your sister in Jerusalem. She is in danger." They prayed and God spared the sister's life. She was spared because she moved when God told her to move and because the couple prayed when God told them to pray.

Power In Your Hand

My Own Life Was Spared

I contracted typhoid fever in Uganda in 1968. One of the faithful sisters in our Richmond church received a dream from God. God showed her that I was sick and dying in Pakistan. Because of that dream the church prayed; and, because they prayed, God spared my life. God delivered me. That faithful sister was available to God.

Mother and I and my two nieces were coming home from a tent meeting in Richmond in 1973. It was just before midnight on a Friday night in June. We were coming north on Interstate 95. School was out, and the highways were crowded.

All three of the others went to sleep. Then, after awhile, I fell asleep too. But I was supposed to be driving.

When I hit the guard rail, I woke up, yanked the wheel, and went back across the highway in the opposite direction–totally out of control. I went through the median strip dividing the north- and southbound traffic. I came out of the median strip and went on over onto the southbound lane in the third traffic lane going south. And I was still headed north.

Mother and I were sure we were going to hit another car head-on. We saw so many lights coming

Availability

toward us that it seemed impossible to miss a collision. When I finally got the car under control, we were just a few inches off the highway. The motor was still running. Mother was in great pain. Her heart had been jammed from all the bouncing on the median strip, but by the mercies of God, we were still alive.

No cars stopped or even slowed up. I got out to see if the car was still in condition to move. Then I said, "Mother, if we don't get out of here, they will kill us." I drove a mile up the southbound lane trying to find a place to cross back to the other side. When I found it, we went on home.

That night, a friend of ours in California, Rev. Confidence Klotz, suddenly got a burden and began to pray. The burden consumed her. She could not stand it. She walked all through her house praying. She said, "God, I don't know the details, but I know that someone is in danger." She opened the back door and went out in her yard. She looked to the heavens; and, turning to the north, the south, the east and the west, said, "Someone is in danger. Spare their lives," she interceded before God.

A day or two later I called Pastor Klotz to tell her about the accident. She asked what time it had happened. I said, "It happened between eleven and eleven thirty at night.

She said, "That would be between eight and eight

thirty at night here in California. I felt it. I could not stand it. I thought I would die. I began to travail in prayer."

I believe that I am alive and my mother is alive because someone was available–someone who could touch God. Somebody knew that another believer was in need. Make yourself available to share the burden of others in these last days.

The Cares of This Life

God is doing unusual things. He is getting us ready for revival. The greatest "ingathering" that we have ever seen is about to take place. It will come to those who are available to the work of the Lord.

Some folks are so caught up with the cares of this life. They will tell you how much they love Jesus, how much they want to be used of God. The cares of this world, however, have so overtaken them, that, when you ask them to do something for God, they answer, "I'm so sorry! I have to do this. I am sorry! I have to do the other thing." What they "have to do" usually doesn't amount to a hill of beans. The devil has made them feel that the natural cares of this life are more important then doing

Availability

the will of God and being available for what God would have them to do.

When God passes them by and picks up a little "nobody" that has half the ability, raises them up and uses them, they wonder why they got bypassed. I don't wonder why. I know why. It is because they are unavailable when God needs someone on the job.

The Lord is looking for men and women that will say, "Yes, God, I am available. I am available. I am available."

My Fear of Preaching In India

On those trips to India in 1961 and 1962, God opened tremendous doors for Mother, Dad and Ruth. They came back telling how that each one preached a full length sermon in every service. Those Indian folks walked miles and miles to get to those conventions. They didn't have to rush back to their jobs. They had come to sit and listen to the Word of God. Each service lasted four or five hours–with at least two preachers. Crowds ranged from five to twenty thousand.

After I heard their testimony, I began praying, "Please, Lord, don't send me to India. I couldn't preach that long." (Seriously, I could only preach about twenty or twenty-five minutes in those days. Since then, I have gotten a little more long-winded.)

Mercifully, God did send me to India in 1969 and do you know what I found out? It is not how long you preach. It is your availability for the anointing of God to flow through you when you lay your hands on the heads of those that are bound by the powers of darkness. When people are getting free from the devil's power, they don't care whether you preach or not. If you are in contact with the throne of Heaven, that's enough.

Make yourself available for the anointing to pour through you. That is what the world is looking for. The world is waiting for YOU to come and give to them what God has already given to YOU. Deliverance comes through the anointing that God gives YOU when YOU are available.

Women, Rise Up

Women, the traditions of men will kill you. Many people still say, "Women, you can't preach! The Law forbade it." But don't you know that Jesus came to fulfill the Law?

When Jesus first came preaching, He came only to *"the lost sheep of the house of Israel,"* only to Jews.

Availability

No Jew would accept a woman preacher; so, Jesus called twelve men. When the work got too big for those twelve He called seventy; and they were all men. They were sent only *"to the lost sheep of the house of Israel."*

Now, however, the commission is:

Go ye into all the world and preach the Gospel TO EVERY CREATURE. ... These signs shall follow THEM THAT BELIEVE.
Mark 16:15 and 17

This commission is to every believer. This *"ye"* includes women and *"then that believe"* includes women.

Jesus called men AND WOMEN to the upper room for the first Holy Ghost ordination service. There He gave them ALL power–the WOMEN included. He commissioned them to go into all the world and baptize–men and WOMEN.

Women, keep yourselves available to do the work that God has called you to do. We need every man and every woman that we can get today who will make themselves available to proclaim the news that Jesus is about to return.

In a national conference in Washington, D.C., Paul Yonggi Cho, Pastor of the world's largest church located in Seoul, Korea, told us that he now has fifty thousand cell-group leaders. Of the fifty thousand, forty-seven thousand are women. He said, "If you have a job you want done, give it to a woman." Hear me, women! Get ready! God is using women today.

Uncle Bill Goes to Colombia

My uncle, Dr. William A. Ward, has fourteen years of college training. He has two Ph.D.s. He has also received several honorary doctorates. In the world's eyes, he has all the right qualifications. He has preached in all the fifty states and in about forty or fifty foreign countries. At one time he had the second largest tent in America, the tent that the famous Jack Coe used. He pastored for a while very successfully in Tulsa, Oklahoma.

Dr. Ward moved to Richmond and pastored a church. Later, he resigned his pastorate and returned to the evangelistic field where he continues today, at 82, blessing multitudes.

At one point, however, he found his preaching schedule empty. It troubled him and he began talking to God about it. He said, "God, I am available for service. Your Word says, *'The harvest is white and the labourers are few.'* You said, *'Pray for the Lord of the harvest to send forth laborers.'* I am available. If

Availability

You don't send me, then You'll have to change Your Word."

That happened on a Sunday afternoon. He went to Mother and Dad's church that night. Ruth, my sister, knew nothing about his talk with God in the afternoon; but when he went up on the platform, she laid hands on him and started to prophesy.

The Holy Ghost said, "Before one week has passed your feet will be on foreign soil to do My bidding." God sees and knows what we speak–even in the secret chambers.

Dad and I, with a team of nine, were conducting a crusade in the coliseum in Bogota, Colombia and God spoke to my uncle to join us. He didn't even have all the expense money he needed; but he prepared himself and went to the airport. At the airport God gave him the balance he needed. He took the plane from Richmond to Miami, then stood in line at the Colombian Airline counter to get a ticket.

The agent said, "I'm sorry! The plane is full."

"Look," Dr. Ward said to the man, "I really have to get to Bogota."

"But, sir, we're full. There are absolutely no seats."

My uncle continued to pester him. He was in and out and back and around that counter, but the man insisted, "I told you there are absolutely no seats available."

Dr. Ward prayed, "God, You know this is Sunday. This is the last plane that I can catch to be on foreign soil to fulfill the prophetic word that You gave me last Sunday." And he stayed right there believing God for a miracle.

When the last passenger arrived to check through the ticket counter, the agent, noticing that he had only a one-way ticket asked to see the man's visa. When the man replied that he had none, the agent explained to him, "The law is that I cannot let you on that plane unless you have either a return ticket from Colombia or a visa."

"I have neither," the man said.

"Then I'm sorry, but I can't let you go," the agent replied.

My uncle was standing right there. The agent said, "Preacher, where is your ticket?"

"Here's my ticket," he said, "and I want to show you a card that I have been holding in my hand." He held it out for the agent to read. It said "EXPECT A MIRACLE." Hallelujah!

Before the seven days were up, his feet were on foreign soil. He did a fantastic job for God as the morning speaker in that coliseum meeting. Five thousand people attended that meeting, and wonderful things happened for God. He stayed on in

Availability

Bogota and continued the meetings after we had gone. Thousands of people were healed and blessed.

Make Yourself Available Now

My friend, if you are available to God, He will open a door and send you. He has methods and means that you and I do not understand.

When we say, "Yes, Lord, I am available," we can forget what people say, what the church says, what the organization says. Forget what everyone says. Just keep yourself on fire for God and watch God open the door and thrust you forth.

We are living in glorious hours. Make yourself available to God and learn His perfect will for you.

When we are not available, we lose the blessing God has planned for us. We are sometimes tossed to and fro between the one thing and the other thing that we are doing. We are not sure whether to give something up or not. We are not sure whether it is the right time to act. We are not sure that we should leave a job or that we should invest our time and energies in a certain obligation and responsibility.

When we keep ourselves available to God, it is easy for Him to speak to us and show us His will.

And when we get to the place that the greatest thing in our lives is to do His will, it is easier to hear the voice of God. We don't want to take one step out of place.

The Scriptures say:

> *As many as are led by the Spirit of God, they are the sons of God.* Romans 8:14

The Lord is leading His people so that we might fulfill the commission He has given us. Be available.

My Prayer For You

Let me pray for you right now. God is right there with you and will help you if you will just believe Him. Let's pray together:

Dear God,

In the Name of Jesus, may the words that we have written here pierce hearts. Help us to lay aside the weights and the sin that so easily beset us and help us to run the race with patience, looking unto Jesus, the Author and Finisher of our faith—Who for the joy that was set before Him endured the cross, despising the shame and is now seated at the right hand of the Father, just waiting to make intercession for us.

God, send forth the challenge to the hearts of Your people everywhere, that they will recognize the power and authority You have given us, that they will be willing to use what they have so that You can do miracles for them, that they will be willing to go where You call them and do what You bid them. Help them to lay aside everything of the flesh, everything of the natural, everything that would hinder Your perfect will in their lives.

We pray, Lord, that Your people will make themselves available to You, that they may not allow the enemy to trick them so that they are set aside on a shelf. May they not do foolish things that will bring sickness in their own bodies.

May they be available at all times to go: to go across the street to their neighbor, to go to another town or to go to the ends of the earth. Whatever the job is that You need done, God, may they be found faithful to perform it.

And, God, I believe right now for a new and fresh call to come upon their lives. Let each one say, "Yes, God, here I am. I am available for service—to do that which would be pleasing in Your sight."

I thank you for your anointing which is going through each one who reads these words and is ministering to their needs. Lord, may they hear and know Your voice and be ready to do Your perfect will.

We give You praise and glory.

> *In Jesus' Name,*
> *AMEN!*

Now, go forth with God's power in YOUR hand to bless those around you.

I beseech you therefore, brethren, by the mercies of God, that ye present your bodies a living sacrifice, holy, acceptable unto God, which is your reasonable service. And be not conformed to this world: but be ye transformed by the renewing of your mind, that ye may prove what is that good, and acceptable, and perfect, will of God. Romans 12:1-2

Calvary Pentecostal Camp

10 1/2 Weeks of SUMMER CAMPMEETING every summer

Campmeeting begins the last Friday of June and continues daily through Labor Day.

**Three great services every day:
11 AM, 3 PM, and 8 PM**

For more information, write us at:

**Ruth Heflin
CPT**
*11352 Heflin Lane
Ashland, VA 23005*

Or call:

(804) 798-7756
Fax. (804) 752-2163

Come and meet God at the camp!